ANGER OVERCOME

Understanding and Managing Anger

BY LINDA CHATELAIN

Special Thanks

A special thank you to my parents, who have always listened patiently and given me strength, no matter which side of anger I have found myself on.

Special Thanks

TABLE OF CONTENTS

Introduction

During the past few days the subject of anger and anger management has been a subject of major discussion and thought. I have thought about all the aspects of anger and how it affects the people it touches. I am thankful for the opportunity to reflect on what I have learned and experienced throughout my life.

In just a few weeks I have been reminded how anger rips apart families, touching everyone within and close around. It causes complete strangers to mourn over happenings they had no control over but are the victims of. Anger affects relationships and positions in the workplace. Worst of all it hurts the person who holds onto anger or uses it as a tool. The person who is angry looks for ways to bring control and peace back into his or her life. Some attempt to use violence, others choose silent revenge. Many choose a life of addiction in some form to food, drugs, alcohol or whatever will dull the ache, bringing them a few moments of forgetfulness and a feeling of power. Others simply allow anger to simmer under the surface until it erupts all over everywhere, everything and everyone around.

Several recent incidents have assisted me in recognizing how anger affects not only those who are angry, but also those who the anger is directed toward or are influenced by the anger between one another. I have witnessed how anger of even one person can affect the lives and decisions of numerous others, adults and children alike. During the past few days the subject of anger, how we react to anger from others or how we manage our own anger have given me an opportunity to look at myself and those around me. One daughter during the past few weeks had to deal with an upheaval in her life and prepare a defense regarding her financial choices over the past four years. I have listened to another daughter promise me if I do not do as she thinks I should she will fight me in court and prove she can control me and get whatever she wants. She will then uproot her children once again to show me my lack of going along with exactly what she asks, as she asks, means I will never see my grandchildren again. She doesn't appear to care how it will affect her children, for she is determined to let me know of her anger and that she can never forgive me for what she believes I have already done to her. I have been able to listen to three children vent their anger concerning decisions of judges, policemen and their own parents regarding the fairness of the legal system. At the same time I have dealt with my own mixed feelings about judges who release men and women from jail with a requirement to complete programs the judges have already sentenced the offender to fulfill several times before, especially when the judge knows part of the reason these people are before them again is they didn't previously complete the programs the last four times they were instructed to. I have experienced my own anger with a therapist canceling yet another session with the children he is supposed to be working with and the resultant tears of disappointment from the children. As the children and I have managed these changes and disappointments in life, we have learned together what is appropriate behavior and what is not. Anger ripples through and touches every member of a family if not recognized and handled in positive ways. Even a five-year-old has pointed out to me how anger can easily be passed from one family member to another. On the other hand recognizing and stopping the anger when it first appears and changing it immediately is passed in hugs and extra efforts of showing love from one to another.

As I have watched and pondered many questions have come to mind. I certainly don't have all the answers but I have learned a few lessons that assist me and make a difference in the choices I make. I certainly don't pretend to be an expert. I am just a normal person living life from day to day the same way you are. Perhaps, in some way sharing the lessons and thoughts I have experienced will assist you to reflect on how anger, has an effect on your life. Perhaps even one thought will hit a chord of truth in your mind to assist in making a positive change in your life. You may find something will help you find more patience with someone who is angry. You may find your own feelings reflected through mine and know you are not alone in your particular situation.

I ask only one thing of you. Knowledge is only of worth when it is shared. So if you find anything of value within these pages I urge you to use it. After you use it and believe it for yourself, share your own thoughts and experiences with others. Pass your positive beliefs along to someone you love and respect. Bless someone you love and want a better relationship with by making a change in yourself they will notice. When they ask what is different about you, share the

4

greatness of positive changes and self-reflection so they can experience along with you more happiness in life.

Defining Anger

Miriam Webster's Collegiate Dictionary, 10th edition, defines anger as "a feeling of displeasure and usually of antagonism." Anger is often used interchangeably with such words as fury, rage, indignation and wrath which all mean an intense emotional state induced by displeasure. Anger, which is the most general term, names the common reaction but in itself conveys nothing about the intensity, justification or manifestation of the emotions felt. Ire is more frequently used in many literary contexts and suggests a greater intensity than anger and often includes an evident display of feeling. Rage suggests a loss of self-control from the violence and passion of the emotion. Fury is an intense, disordered and often-destructive rage that sometimes seem completely out of control. The word indignation stresses the feeling of righteous anger concerning what one considers unfair, mean or shameful. Wrath is used most often to suggest a desire or intent to take revenge or to seek retribution and punishment as a way of expressing feelings.

For simplicity in our discussion I am going to use the term anger to describe any of these feelings and reactions. As a general term it will work for understanding that anger is a reaction. Words such as fury, rage and wrath describe well the depths of the reactions to the true issues involved.

Anger is defined as a feeling of hate, hurt, frustration or fear. Anger is an emotional reaction to the physical and chemical changes of the body that prepare a person to fight or run. Anger is a mix of feelings that is different for everyone. Most generally it is a deep feeling of reaction of wanting to fight in some way because of something we perceive as unfair, uncalled for, unnecessary, hurtful or threatening. Anger is a secondary reaction to that deeper feeling underneath. Anger is a reaction to, a symptom or a façade for what we are really feeling.

According to Leonard Ingram, Anger Institute of Chicago, Daryl Dowsing M.A. explained the typical sequence of anger. "First, a "trigger," usually a situation or a statement made by another person, sets you off. Then a thought, or series of thoughts ("Why is she so mean?" "What did I ever do to him?"), followed by a belief about those thoughts ("This is so unfair" or "She doesn't love me"), and the feeling (hurt, betrayal) that accompanies those beliefs. After all that thinking, or "self-talk," as many therapists call it, comes the behavior, either overt actions like blowing up, shouting, hitting or breaking objects, or inward actions like sulking and pouting."[1]

Anger is a reaction to natural human emotions we often experience. An emotion is a deep feeling about something true in our experience. Anger involves a surge of energy which gives you the desire to act in relation to whatever you perceive is wrong or upsets you. Anger is typically experienced as an almost automatic response to other feelings. It is a secondary reaction to a much deeper feeling underneath usually not even recognized as the real reason for what we are feeling. We feel the resultant anger without looking for the reasons or asking ourselves why. Anger is a reaction to, a symptom or a façade for what we are really feeling.

Anger is also a natural step in the process of grief. . Most people who are working through the feelings of grief must go through a phase of feeling angry because of their loss. The loss could be a treasured loved one or a diagnosed illness. The steps of grief are a part of dealing with a loss of employment, a divorce or separation, the loss of a home or a move away from valuable friends and family.

Identifying Anger

Identifying anger is important. It is a problem faced by every culture and in every country. Anger affects everyone at one time or another. Understanding your own anger and the anger of others allows you to seek tools to arm yourself with. Understanding and identifying what anger is and why people choose to express or feel the various depths of anger helps you recognize and deal with anger more quickly and efficiently. If you understand the phases of anger,

---

[1] http://www.stimes.com/News/102099/Floridian/Controlled_burn_shtml

the types of anger and the expressions of anger, you are much more likely to choose different ways of dealing with your own or others feelings and show of emotion.

Identifying anger can be as easy as identifying physical changes in either our own bodies and minds or the expressions and actions of someone else. Anger is an emotional reaction to the physical and chemical changes of the body that prepare a person to fight or run. When we are angry we are prepared to act. Our bodies produce certain physiological reactions such as increased levels of adrenaline in the blood stream, an increased heart rate, rapid but shallow breathing, dilated pupils, sweating of the palms and a tight feeling in the chest. When we experience anger we often have a difficult time remaining still. This increase in energy makes it difficult for the body and mind to relax and problems in sleeping are common. The word "anger" says nothing about any justification, duration or intensity with respect to the emotion. Anger becomes a problem when it gets out of control, when it consumes a person's energy. In this state, behaviorally, the angry person usually makes poor choices. This often leads to negative effects, such as verbal and/or physical aggression with the attendant negative consequences.

Sometimes anger can be identified by the unconscious physical reactions of someone who is struggling with what to do about their angry reaction. It is not uncommon for a person to clench their fists in an effort to stay calm. They may talk through clenched teeth and tight lips moving their mouths as little as possible. They may furrow their brow or close their eyes to maintain a semblance of control. Anger is easily identified in the parent with hands on hips and a scowl on their face. The person who is pounding on the desk or punches a hole in the wall without even thinking is probably one who is dealing with the reactions of anger. An angry child often stomps his foot and shouts out his feelings making sure that he is heard. The raised voice and pointing finger are generally accepted by society as a sign of anger and control. These are only just a sampling of behaviors that indicate the presence of anger in a relationship or situation.

Sometimes though, it is not as easy to identify a reaction of anger. Some people get very adept at hiding behind a calm face while hormones and energy are seething and simmering below. They have developed walls and masks that protect them and serve to keep those who might think of assisting them at a distance. They may keep calm, but keep their arms crossed to guard themselves from other hurt. They may take a stance of standing while you are sitting because they feel more in control. There are far too many people that can remain calm in the situation where anger is triggered but react later. A common example would be the man who does not let his boss at work know that he is offended or challenged but once at home releases the pent-up energy of anger by abusing his wife or children or making unreasonable demands that can never be achieved. Think about the obedient student in school that always appears in class with a smile on his face and an outreached hand to others but beyond the doors steals, shoplifts and blackmails others to support his current drug addiction only his closest friends are aware of. Some people show more of their fear than their anger. They cower beneath the rod of scorn and abuse, always staying for more; afraid of changing the balance they have come to live with as their victim calling in life.

Types of Anger

Anger generally can be classified as falling within one of five types of anger. These types of anger are: anger at others; other's anger at us; anger at something from the past (usually something that remains unresolved); abstract anger (raging at fate and life in general, the proverbial "chip on the shoulder"); and anger at yourself. While each one of these types can stand alone, and may be the beginning reaction, many times a person is dealing with a combination of these. They may be angry at themselves for allowing something to happen that reminds them of a past experience or a person from their past. In experiencing the present occurrence all the feelings of the past are felt as strongly as they were before. The anger at others in the past may cloud a person's perception of the intent of those that are part of the present. Even when a person is feeling a combination of types of anger, he will generally focus on one type of anger in which to express himself.

Anger at others is the most recognized type of anger that I have found people associate with. Anger at others is justified, sustainable and even empowering. Being angry with someone else makes the angry person feel like he has a little more control. He is able to focus his attention and energy in one direction outside of himself. To keep anger fueled he focuses on the feelings of hurt and unfairness that he perceives he received. Blame is one of the most common reactions involved when anger at another person is the type of anger chosen. Blaming someone else allows the angry person to release responsibility. Blame is necessary in order not to feel anger towards self or believe there could have been a different outcome. Anger at others keeps the pain and hurt at a distance. It is so much easier to be angry with someone else than it is to think about what we are really feeling. As long as the focus can be kept on anger at others the person experiencing the anger does not have to feel the pain, hurt, frustration or disappointment triggering the emotion or feeling they are reacting to. Putting their thoughts into revenge, retaliatory actions or acts of control keeps the person actively focused outside of them.

People choose into anger every day. We cannot live in this world of human beings without at some time offending someone else or experiencing the anger of others directed to us. Having someone's anger directed at us is a double-edged experience. On one side we feel the effects of their anger. We experience their anger expressed and directed toward us in the form of mean or derogatory words, actions and thoughts. We know the results of revenge, hate, physical or emotional abuse or even threats of physical harm. We feel pain as they may withdraw their affection, support or approval if they feel it is valuable to us. We suffer a loss as their anger requires a price from us. On the other side, we also may feel anger in return. If we do not feel they are justified or fair in their anger we also experience anger towards them and a desire to make them understand our side or to hurt back in return. Dealing with one type of anger is hard enough. Having to fluctuate from the feeling of one type of anger to another can sometimes seem overwhelming. Confusion and an inability to make decisions easily are not uncommon when dealing with anger from others.

Everyone has a past, a yesterday. No one has made it to today without something happening yesterday to make them who they are today. Decisions made by others and by ourselves have paved the path to where we are today. How we perceive and deal with these past experiences varies from person to person. While we may accept and live with most people, experiences, opportunities and happenings in our past, there are some that may still have an effect on our lives. Past choices may influence our freedom, our abilities or the even the way people treat us in the present. As reminders come up about the past some people feel as angry now as they might have then. They may never have gotten over their anger and so each time something triggers a memory or similar instances occur, anger jumps quickly to the surface. An adult who was abused as a child may unconsciously feel anger whenever anyone they perceive as an authority questions their actions or responds to them in anything other than complete acceptance. The child, who never forgave her father for abandoning her, carries that anger into her relationships with her husband and sons as an adult. The parent whom the child was angry at as a teen for throwing him out because of inappropriate behavior reacts with just as much anger as an adult when given the same choice to either leave or change. When someone is angry because of something they experienced in the past, particularly something they have not overcome or learned a new way of living with, they often are experiencing feelings of inferiority or powerlessness. Their present day reaction is generally to try to control, to change the present so it does not resemble the past. They may act out to prove that they are powerful or in control, hurting not only themselves but also all around them. They may try to prove that this time they won't get caught, this time it is different. The opposite anger response is to re- repress the feelings, deny that they are feeling the pain or the hurt. They may have done it successfully for a time once before and it worked for a while. In order to repress the feelings, these people live in a world where reality does not exist. Trying to avoid the anger from the past some may choose to control their anger or change their perception by turning to drugs or alcohol to dull the pain.

Almost everyone at one time or another is angry at life in general. The news, good and bad, is that life is not always fair. Life does not always match our dreams and desires. Life goes on whether we are ready for it or not. So it is natural that there will be times when what happens in life will trigger a feeling within we choose to express through the faces of anger. Some people walk around with a "chip on their shoulder" just waiting for someone or something to knock it off balance. They will sometimes even walk around asking in one way or another for someone to knock off the chip because then they can get angry, they can allow their anger to be directed at someone or focused toward a specific time and place instead of just sitting under the surface waiting to erupt. A person who is simply angry at life many times has a deep belief that life should be fair, everyone should be equal and everyone should have the same shot at life. When life is not the way they envisioned or they receive a setback they don't know how to move on. They may not have the coping skills to be able to move in a different direction, make a different choice or be open to the possibility that this new change could be even better than what they are waiting for. So they sit and wait for life to happen according to their fantasy. They can't feel anything else, so they choose to just be angry at life in general or the cards fate has dealt them. On the opposite end of the line is the person who needs to prove that their perception of life is right. They head out to rebel against life, against society, against parents. They have something to prove about life and anybody that gets in their way is going to be hurt, run-over, eliminated or thrown away. They may shoplift or steal because they feel they deserve or are entitled to what they see others have. They may steal or shoplift just to show that they can do it and not have to pay the price everyone else does or to see how many times they can get away with it without being caught. Those that are angry at life may join the ever increasing organizations that are determined that life should be a certain way and are willing to do whatever it takes to create their vision or punish anyone between them and their vision, including possibly dying themselves in order to make someone else believe the strength of their convictions.

The fifth type of anger commonly experienced is anger at self. I think this is sometimes the hardest type of anger to experience and choose. Anger at self-hurts. There is no way to feel anger towards self without feeling pain inside. It involves judging ourselves as unworthy of love, of kindness or of understanding for something we believe, have believed or perceived we experienced. Anger at self follows the feelings of guilt, being responsible, sorrow or grief. When there is no one else to blame or be angry at then the only one left to direct the feelings of loss or hurt towards is self. Acceptance is one of the most basic human needs so if we do not accept our own actions as lovable, the feeling of hurt and betrayal surfaces. If we do not like this feeling or do not understand it or judge the feeling as wrong we choose into a feeling of anger to replace the feeling of hurt or the pain of betrayal to ourselves. When anger is directed inward it seeks a place to hide. This is the type of anger that is repressed and hidden from others. We deny the feelings and refuse to confront the issues that are causing the pain. In doing so our anger increases even more. Anger does not stay buried for long. By its nature it surfaces in one form or another. When it surfaces it appears in feelings of revenge, rebelliousness, a desire to hurt/punish or a lack of support. Just as these can be directed outward when the focus is external, these same expressions can be turned inward against ourselves. We may want to run away. We can do it physically or emotionally. We hide from the world behind our addictions, within our safety zones. We put up walls that no one can get past and lash out if anyone tries to get near. We find ways of proving to ourselves over and over that the anger is warranted, deserved and keep on punishing ourselves for past mistakes we cannot forgive ourselves for. Anger at self results too many times in "dis-ease" within the body and mind. Self-punishment surfaces in disorders such as anorexia or bulimia. It may surface in the macho male who craves the risk of proving how often he can get hurt or crash and still keep walking away. It may show its face in chronic illnesses that have no medical basis but are still real. It shows up in the drug addict or the alcoholic who keeps needing a bigger or a longer high and feeling of control. Sadly there are those who cannot deal with this anger turned inward. They decide that the pain is too great, the fight too hard or the battle cannot be won and express their anger by making one last cry, choosing death over life.

Expressions of Anger

How anger is expressed can be either positive or negative. Most generally we find that anger is expressed in negative ways. I have identified in myself and others a number of ways that anger is expressed.

12

Aggression is a common reaction to anger. Shoving, slapping hitting or kicking are common actions. Some people throw or break things, rationalizing it is a more acceptable behavior because they are not causing physical harm to another person. Others may be verbally abusive, resorting to yelling, name calling, insulting or swearing.

Criticism is another form of a verbal expression of anger. Criticism may be pointed in the direction of a situation, a person or sometimes even toward personal behavior.

Some people express anger through vengeful behavior. They may threaten to "get even" or declare "you won't get away with this." The common feeling behind vengeful behavior is a desire to get back at someone who has made them feel victimized, humiliated, taken advantage of or violated in some way.

Sarcastic remarks can often be traced to a feeling of anger. Sarcastic people may be trying to embarrass or humiliate as a way of being vengeful. Making a joke at someone else's expense or poking fun at someone, although not physically harmful, is still a way of using anger to impact another person in a negative manner.

Willfully withdrawing from communicating with someone is another way expressing anger. Rather than lashing out verbally or physically, some people choose to become silent. Refusing to talk or communicate is a way of expressing their belief that their anger is justified. It may, at times also be a way of trying to express to another that the anger is so deep that there is no way the other person can rectify what has been done.

Another, often silent, expression of anger is in the withdrawal of something of value, usually something we are sure the other person wants, needs or desires. It may be a withdrawal of time, money, assistance or support. It may take the form of forgetting or refusing to participate in normal routines or performances. I may be even be a refusal of affection, caring or love in a relationship.

Mismanaged Anger

How anger is managed has an affect not only the person experiencing the anger, but all those that are around. Anger managed in a either a negative or a positive way affects families, neighbors and friends. How anger is managed affects those in the workplace, schools and other places in society where we meet and mingle one with another.

Controlled anger, short-term and targeted at a specific object or person may be helpful and healthy, as in the case of parenting an errant child or a non-performing student. Controlled anger, used in a positive way, may give someone the extra energy or incentive to try something different, something new or adventurous. Controlled anger is useful in helping people to direct their focus and actions in appropriate ways such as in the case of natural or forced emergencies and disasters. The rescuer, pushed by anger at the elements, pushes that much harder to reach the victim. The anger of an official may be what triggers offers of support and assistance to victims of abuse or criminal actions.

It is the manifestation of uncontrolled, inappropriate anger that we hear about and read about every day. The results of uncontrolled, inappropriate anger are often destructive. In most cases, becoming agitated and terribly aroused ultimately produces a loss of focus, purpose, and momentum, frequently leading to negative consequences such as fatigue and confusion. The display of excessive anger may serve to induce fear in the minds of those around them, serving as a barrier to open communication and genuine love. The expressions of anger may be inappropriate with respect to the type and intensity with regard to the situation. It is not uncommon enough for someone to use the hammer to kill a fly because his or her perception of reality is not clear.

The results of anger touch the lives of families as homes become torn apart or broken through the expressions of anger. Anger is felt by the abused child or the battered spouse who cannot or will not leave the situation. Anger that cannot be overcome leads couples to the divorce courts and creates single parent homes where children do not have the influence of both a mother and father. Anger continues sometimes to affect lives long after the papers are signed when the separated individuals still have confrontations over children, responsibilities and choices. Years after anger has separated a family, a single parent will still feel the extra feelings of being both mother and father and making daily decisions alone.

The symptoms of disease and addictions affect much more the person that is diagnosed as the owner. Caregivers and co-dependents suffer along with them. Family members support them because it is sometimes easier and less time consuming to give in to the demands of the disease than to fight. Repressed anger that shows up in depression and fatigue mean there may be children that need to care for themselves or other siblings and act as adults while their childhood passes them by. The child who lives with depression loses his own faith in life, giving up hope as life spirals downward around him. Every family member is affected when the money that should buy food and warm clothing is used to purchase the drugs, alcohol and medications that allow the addict to maintain some semblance of control of life and self. When the calm can be found life may be good, but when the need is not met, life becomes treacherous and unpredictable for those nearby and for the person suffering.

We commonly read in the papers and hear on the daily news the violent actions of people who were overcome by anger. The angry motorist shoots at the driver of a passing car for following too closely. We read about the many lives torn asunder by the frustration of a few teens that shot their friends at a local high school. We listen to the news of workers frustrated by unemployment as more and more companies downsize that vandalize businesses. We find out that the fire that destroyed hundreds of nearby homes was purposely set by the business owner unable to recover from lost business when the new discount warehouse opened around the block. One reporter tells of the casualties of the latest terrorist bombing in his country while another reporter reports on the latest toll in wounded civilians caught in the explosions of war in another. Meanwhile stores raise their prices to recoup the loss from theft and shoplifting as more and more people are turned away from benefit programs for the unemployed.

Mismanaged or unmanaged anger demands a price. The costs are high in lost income, broken relationships, loss of jobs, damage to property and other people, financial hardships and destroyed lives. The list is as unique as the individuals that experience anger. Everyone that experiences anger creates their own results that works for them in their own circles of life.

Taking the Steps to Management

It is possible to manage anger. Many people do it every day. It is not impossible, though at times it may feel that way. To some people remaining calm and not reacting to feelings, emotions and situations in life that challenge their perceptions or beliefs comes easily. For most of the rest of us, it takes effort and thought. It takes stopping and recognizing what is happening, asking why and making a decision of what to do or feel next.

Learning to manage anger is not an overnight activity or miracle. It requires an everyday effort. It begins today, in this moment. Are you ready to begin? Yes. You have already begun by reading this today. You have already made the decision to choose something different, to look for another idea or to find something new to learn. So I will journey on with you and take your hand. I'll continue sharing some of the lessons I have learned over my many years of life and you listen for that inner voice that says to you, this could be true, this could work.

Stop, Look and Listen

Stop. Simply stop. This is one of the first ways of managing the feelings and actions of anger. Stop, look and listen is a concept we learn as children in kindergarten. It is no less important to use as an adult, as we grow

Stop and take a deep breath. Let your body, mind and thoughts stop where they are for just a moment. Some people suggest counting to ten. Others suggest taking ten breaths before talking. On the road a stop sign keeps traffic under control. It allows traffic to flow, for people to take turns. The direction to stop is meant to avoid accidents from happening, from people getting hurt because of narrow vision.   Stop before the collision begins. Stop and let the other person go first. Stop and watch for danger before proceeding. Is this where you want to go? Do you need to change directions? Do you need to slow down?   Stop and make a decision about the next thought, the next word, and the next action you want to take. Will it get you what you want? Will it get you where you want to go in this relationship or situation?

Look both ways before crossing the street.   It is a simple childhood safety tip. As we grow do we use the direction or lesson in our lives? Look at yourself. Are you who and what you want to be? Do you see a person you like? Are you a person other people can like? Step back and look both ways before you proceed full steam ahead on your personal track. Are there others coming toward you that may need to wait to pass? Is there a situation coming your way that you can learn from or you want to be a part of? Look to the side and see if there is more information coming your way from a different direction than the way you are headed that will be of benefit to you. Look within and ask yourself questions? How are you feeling? What are you doing? Why are you proceeding with or without caution toward your next decision, your next word or your next action?

Listen. Listen to yourself, to others and to the air around you. Are others saying something you should be listening to? Are you saying what it is you want to say? Do you hear yourself merely spouting out meaningless words or are you expressing what you really feel? When you listen to the other person, what do you hear? Listen for the feeling or meaning behind the words, not just the words alone. Are you even listening or are you caught up in your own emotions and thoughts? Listen to learn and understand. Listen more for the love spoken instead of listening to hear something to be offended by.   What are the sounds you hear around you? Is there peace or discord in the air? Do you hear others laughing and happy or do you hear them repeating your anger and passing it on?   Listen to the silence of a moment and the beat of your heart. Listen to the voices screaming within to be heard as well as the ones to be silenced.

Recognize the Choice

As we go through life we experience the energy of life within us and around us. The energy we experience becomes thought. Based on the thoughts we form we learn to make choices, to decide between two possibilities. As we make more choices we form patterns in our life that either do or do not work for us on a personal level. If we change our perceptions, our thoughts, we change the choices we can make, and we change our life.

Anger is not a natural feeling. It is a reaction we choose in response to other emotions.   Anger is not something that happens; it is something that we choose to feel. . It is a stance or a feeling we choose because it keeps us energized, focused or motivated to do something different, to make a change in some way or make a change in others. Anger is the defense we choose in order not to face our real feelings or the reaction to the feeling we don't want to take the time to examine and work through right now. Anger is a choice to take action or to let someone know of our feelings.   As we experience feelings, interact with people and have various experiences we choose at every turn how we will feel and react. . We can feel sad or happy so we choose to frown or smile. . We can feel afraid and choose to either run or to put on a brave face and face our fears head on. We can feel hurt and still have the choice to show it with tears or put on the smiling face to fool the world.   We can feel one thing at a time, so we can either feel the underlying emotions or we can choose to feel the escalated feeling of anger. It is always a choice.

I cannot count how many times I have heard someone say "He made me so mad." Many a time I have caught myself starting to say "Don't make me mad," as I am trying to stop my child from doing something I have asked him not to. No one can make you angry. Anger is a choice that you make. No one can control how you think, how you feel or what you decide. Everyone is responsible for his own thoughts and actions. No one can make you do anything you do not want to do or feel anything you do not want to feel.   It is always a choice you make. Granted sometimes we choose to feel as someone would like us to in order to avoid something, to please or to just get past the moment as quickly as possible with the least amount of

18

conflict. The same is true with anger. It is always our choice not anyone else's. No one can make you angry. Only you can choose to be angry. No one can make you be revengeful, but you can choose to take revenge on someone. No one can make you use violence to prove your point but if you think it will serve your purpose you may rationalize that force is the answer for you to use.

Because anger is a choice you can be angry or not. It is as simple as that. It is your choice to make. You can choose to step back, learn and move forward in an appropriate manner or we can choose to be angry and vent our emotions inappropriately, unrealistically and just move without learning or accepting our part in the creation of the results you are currently experiencing. Even the rape victim, the, assault victim has a choice to be angry, to forget, to find support or to forgive.

Own the Anger.

Anger is never about the other person. Anger is a personal matter. If you are feeling anger it is never about what someone else did, said or caused to happen. It is always about your own perceptions and reactions. Personal anger is not something that someone chooses for us, it is something we choose to experience and feel ourselves. No one can feel your anger but you. So anger is never about how the other person feels or what the other person did. Anger is always about how you feel personally. Anger is about your skills in dealing with the ups and downs of life as it unfolds. Anger is about how you can or cannot express what you are thinking or believe.

When you can own your own feelings, take responsibility for your own choices, you will find a new release of energy that naturally lifts and sustains you. Even though you may feel the pain and feelings you have been avoiding, your self-esteem magically escalates without any effort on your part. As long as you hide behind blaming others for your circumstances you cannot heal and change what is the real reasons you choose anger. As long as you are busy fanning the flames of anger through blaming others you do not have the energy to make the changes that will keep the annoying situation from happening exactly the same way again. When you begin to own your anger as something belonging to you, you acknowledge that you have a voice in your life. You are not tossed about by fate. You are able to recognize the signs before you pass them and can steer yourself in a different direction to avoid the head-on encounter. When you own and feel the anger as something you created for yourself as a defense you begin to feel. If you can feel you know that you are alive. As long as you are alive you can feel life, experience it and make new choices.

One of these first steps in overcoming or better managing anger is to recognize you have an anger problem. In order to overcome anger you have to realize that anger is where you are functioning. Recognizing and admitting anger may be your motivator, your basis of decisions, your energy of existence or the space you are in. How do you recognize it? You never relax. You don't sleep because the anger interrupts your rest. The same situation keeps revolving in your mind over and over as you seek a different ending. If you are trying to hurt someone else just to hurt then you are probably stuck in anger. Look at the motivations and recognize that you are feeling angry and ask why? If you yell first or lash out in rage before you ask questions, own your anger and admit that you need to make a change. Admit you have a problem with anger management. If you walk around hating life and most of the people in your life for something they have done, said or were a part of, you have the opportunity right now to own your anger problem, to look at it realistically and decide if you want to have different relationships or if you enjoy feeling miserable. Own the results that you have created with your anger. Own your life as you have created it and own the part that anger has made in creating your present circumstances. Were you too angry with someone to accept his or her help or advice? Did your anger assist others in making choices that now affect your life and what you would like it to be? Could it have been different if your anger had not been in the way of your judgments? Take a good hard look at where you are and admit how much anger colors everything you see and feel in this moment.

Identify the Reasons & Issues

The next step in changing how you manage anger is to identify the feelings and issues that are underneath the surface of the anger. Ask yourself the questions only you have the answers to. What is it that you are really angry about? What are you really feeling? What are your attitudes and beliefs that trigger your feelings of anger? Where did they come from? How and when did you decide that life had to be a certain way? Where or when did you feel this way before? What did you do about it then? How did your choice affect your life? Ask and then ask again. You will find that each time you ask your mind will give you a different answer. Listen and learn from the answers you get.

Trigger Feelings of Anger

As discussed before, anger is a reaction to another feeling or emotion that we are experiencing on a deeper level. Anger is the way we choose to deal with the feeling. Anger is the defense against feeling, the protective shield we put up when we feel threatened, or our beliefs are threatened in some way.

One of the major keys to understanding anger is to look for the deeper feeling that we are trying to protect, defend or even deny. Most of the feelings fall into about six general categories. We choose into anger due to a perceived hurt, fear, a feeling of powerlessness, a sense of betrayal, jealousy or frustration. These categories are very general. Within each of them are many other feelings that often go hand-in-hand with the beginning feelings, one feeling leading to another. These six feelings mentioned appear to be the most common feelings that are triggered on the first levels of feeling.

Perceived Hurt

No one likes to be hurt. It doesn't feel good no matter how we pretend that we are not touched by it. If we perceive that someone is hurting us, our bodies automatically start producing chemical and hormones that prepare us to put up a defense. Often times the defense is sustained by the feeling of anger that allows those levels to remain high and constant.

The hurt we experience may be emotional or physical. The hurt could be a mean word, an act of violence or even the result of an accident. What the act was that caused the hurt is seldom the triggering factor. Even how seriously we are physically or emotionally hurt has little to do with the level of our feeling. What is or has been simply is. The critical factor is how we perceive the hurt. Do we see the hurt as something that was intentional? How do we feel about that? Was it something that we felt we had control over? Would we have created a different situation that didn't hurt so much? Do we perceive the hurt as repetitive? Do we perceive the hurt as on a higher level than the last time you felt this way? Have we made choices that we thought would protect us from being hurt but we still got hurt anyway? What experiences and other feelings does this hurt bring to mind? The answers to all these questions and many more are the core of the anger. It is not the hurt itself but our perception of the hurt that makes the difference.

One of the feelings that fall into this area is a feeling someone has treated us unfairly. We feel that we did not deserve the treatment we received. We can recognize this type of trigger when our immediate reaction is the feeling of "How dare you do this to me?" We want to seek revenge, to hurt back, to be able to say or show the other person they can't treat us like this. The person who feels like they have been "stabbed in the back" is experiencing a perceived hurt. You see this type of feeling in the child who does not want to be grounded, and stomps his foot or throws a temper tantrum in order to disturb the peace in the home, to embarrass mother in public or to get attention he feels he is missing.

This sense of being treated unfairly is part of the feeling of grief experienced by the survivors of tragic circumstances. Even if the act was random or the result of something like a fatal disease, sooner or later the question is asked, "Why me?" There is almost always a feeling of being singled out which makes the act seem unfair and uncalled for. The guilt of being left behind brings about the same question, or the question of "Why not me?" It feels lonely to be left behind, unfair to be left to suffer and feel. Asking the questions makes the hurt that much harder to bear, so heavy that anger is the only thing our heart will allow us to feel while it heals. Feeling like we were treated unfairly, the anger towards the person we feel is to blame allows us to focus our energy away from ourselves, to lessen the feelings inside or to put off for a time feeling the emotions.

Anger occurs when we believe that life should be fair for everyone and it doesn't appear as being fair in this instance. It is the limited belief that everyone should have the same number of cookies, chances, opportunities, etc. regardless of any other factors. When someone else gets an extra cookie, or gets something we didn't get then anger is the reaction. Some people simply stomp their feet and say over and over in their loudest voices "It Isn't fair. It isn't fair. Others see it as not fair and work to take away the cookie from the other person they see with more in order to even the field again. But there are others that can stop, quietly say "Life is not fair," look for the lesson and move on without having to prove anything to themselves or to others.

The key to understanding the trigger emotions of perceived hurt is the word perceived. It is the way we look at something based on our past and present experiences and the decisions we have made and beliefs we have formed based upon those experiences. Perception of hurt and the perception of the magnitude of hurt are individual factors. Someone accidentally bumping me while standing in a line may not bother me but the person behind me who has been bumped and pushed all day by coworkers and fellow travelers trying to protect their own spaces my react instantly with an angry word or action, not because he was actually hurt but because he perceived he was hurt. While one person may laugh at the phrase "If you loved me..,you would..." the person who was abused by an accuser may instantly relive the times the phrase was used to manipulate and hurt, feeling the pain all over again and react in a totally different way. Even if the phrase "If you loved me.." was used in jest, the feelings of the past color the present and anger may be directed toward the present speaker simply because the feelings are so painful the only way that has been found to deal with them is to direct them outward. A person who has learned that sometime people say things out of reaction rather than thought is much less likely to feel hurt by an occasional mean word than a person who has grown up with the knowledge that people purposely say things to hurt other people and speak exactly what they think, especially if it is meant to hurt. Perception of hurt, perception of purpose, perception of worth and perception on beliefs all work together to trigger feelings that are expressed through or covered over by anger.

Fear

Fear is a tremendous trigger for anger. I have heard many people describe fear as when "false expectations appear real." Fear is a reaction of both mind and body. When faced with fear the body responds by preparing to face the challenge. The body sets itself for either fight or flight. It is natural to have an emotional feeling to thoughts of "How dare you scare me or threaten me."

Fear of the unexpected or the unwanted can trigger anger to those we feel may bring about the presence of the things we fear. We fear the outcome, usually one that we do not want. We want our lives to stay stable and calm. And we fear the upheaval we think someone else will make or cause. Our belief system is threatened or we feel threatened in some say. We are angry because we know we might have to fight to defend and we really don't want to.

We may be angry because our own fears of failure may be threatened. The student who is angry with the teacher who won't give a clue as to the contents of the test, is really afraid that he will not know the answers he believes he should know. He is afraid of failure and anger is a way of avoiding facing the fear.

Anger is the defense we put up to shield us from the physical and emotion threats and abuse from others. Fear of or a belief that the other person might just be able to do what they say they can is reason enough to feel angry. We put up our guard because we are afraid of the possibility of pain or harm occurring. It is better to be ready than to be taken by surprise.

Anger is triggered for many simply through feeling and thinking about their own personal fears. They feel the fear and choose to be angry with those who do not exhibit the same fears. The anger doesn't have to be based in reality, it only has to be based in belief of possibility. Fear of failure may mean you are angry with those who succeed. Fear of taking a risk may induce anger at those who risk and win. Fear of the unknown may mean someone is angry at those who appear unconcerned with what may or may not happen because of their actions or who it may affect.

Powerlessness

Anger is a reaction to a perceived loss of freedom or rights. The feeling that we are powerless to do whatever, whenever or however we want and we should be allowed to no matter what is the trigger for expressing our desires in a more powerful way. If we are angry, we can fool ourselves into believing at least we are not just sitting idly by without putting up some kind of a fight. It is the belief we should be entitled to freedom even when it hurts or interferes with someone else's freedom or rights and no one should interfere with us. The loss of freedom pushes other feelings to the surface and rather than deal with them we choose to feel anger at being stopped, being kept from something important to us or we strongly desire.

Anger comes from a feeling of being out of control. We react in anger to those who are in a position of authority, who question our power or threaten our chosen positions. Anger is the mask we wear when we feel someone else is making decisions for us we want to make for ourselves, feel we can make for ourselves or wish we could make for ourselves. It is a reaction to feeling powerless in a situation, like there is nothing you can do to make a difference or a change or to change the outcome. Being out of control is not a good feeling no matter how you color it. Giving up the control of our lives to, for or because of someone else triggers the feeling of loss and triggers the beginnings of anger that grow ever deeper. The inmate at a jail or a patient in a hospital often have feelings of a loss of freedom or control that trigger their feelings of anger at a system, a situation or even the people that are trying to assist them.

Sense of Betrayal

Another common trigger for many people is the feeling of being betrayed. We find ourselves saying things like "Look at all I have done" or "After all that I have done you still ..." or "After all I have given how could you..." It is seen in the worker who gives his all at work and does not feel appreciated and begins to feel discontentment growing that develops into anger at his supervisors or coworkers. It is a common trigger for the person passed up for the promotion after giving years of service and watches as someone below him gets the raise, especially if they are then asked to train the new person to fill the position. The mother or father who has given up his or her own wishes and desires to provide for a child who never seems to be grateful is probably feeling a form of this anger because of the hurt they feel at not being appreciated.

Anger is triggered, sometimes quickly, when we feel that trust has been betrayed. This trigger is recognized when we hear the words "I thought I could trust you" or "I expected you to..." or even "I believed that..." Any one of these feelings can be a trigger for anger. The spouse who is unfaithful, the child who disappoints a parent, the parent who doesn't keep a promise and the judge who lets the criminal walk away all are examples of people who may trigger our emotions so strongly that we choose to be angry.

A feeling of betrayal, in any of its forms, is based in an expectation. In looking at the trigger of betrayal, we also get to look at the expectations we have developed throughout our lives. What do we expect of others, ourselves, life in general? Is the sense of betrayal we feel based on realistic or unrealistic expectations? The strength of our expectations greatly affects the depth of our anger and even the length of time we choose to angry.

Jealousy

One side of jealousy is strongly connected to expectations of fairness and equality. Jealousy is a desire to have something you see someone else enjoying. It is a feeling of hurt that you do not have the same. It is a feeling of not wanting to like or be happy for someone because they have what you would like. Since you can't have what you want you search for a way to express your feeling of unfulfilled desire and anger becomes the choice of expression. You hear your self saying things such as "If I had ... I would..." or "If only I had..."or "It's not fair that...has...I should..." This jealousy is dependent on judgments of what is better or less. A person only feels jealous if they perceive that what the other person has is better than what they have themselves. Until the comparison is made the jealousy doesn't occur but once made the jealousy triggers a feeling of inferiority that is expressed in dissatisfaction with circumstances or anger.

There is another side of jealousy that is based in expectations and beliefs about control, ownership and devotion. This type of

26

jealousy triggers anger whenever the expectations are not met. The jealous person believes and expects people involved with them to be true, faithful, dedicated and serving only to them. You see this type of jealousy in the boyfriend who gets angry with his girlfriend because she smiled at another boy as she walked down the hall at school. You see it in the girl who is angry because her best friend chose not to sit by her because she wanted to meet the new girl on the bus. Jealousy and anger in this mode dwell very near each other. This jealousy is a two edged sword that cuts both people involved. Neither person involved in the relationship is untouched by the triggers of anger it inflicts. The person who is jealous gets angry if they do not feel they can trust, control or maintain control of the moments of life of the other person. The other person involved ends up feeling angry because they feel controlled, manipulated, untrustworthy or confused about what is expected of them. No matter which side of this jealousy you are on, the emotions can trigger and explode into anger, often very quickly and sometimes violently.

Frustration

Anger is the reaction to the feeling of frustration. We express anger because things are not going as expected, the way we want or expected them to or waited to happen a certain way and so present events are not meeting our expectations in perfection. Anger is a reaction to our beliefs that something or someone should be a certain way that we want or need them to be to fulfill our needs, wants or wishes. Frustration is a reaction to finding out that all things are not as perfect in a perfect world as we would like them to be.

Frustration is the feeling we feel when after trying and trying again we don't see the progress expected or desired. It is the feeling that life is not moving along, changes are not occurring fast enough for us to feel satisfied or happy. It is felt when you see the bus you were rushing to catch leave the stop seconds before you get there and you have to wait for the next one to come. You feel it when you know you perform your work well in a job position but your scores on the test to get the job are not as good as you would like because you always get nervous when taking a test.   You feel frustration when you know you need to be in one place but would like to be somewhere else doing something else. You may feel frustrated and lose your patience when you are pressured for time and a child is acting his age and playing with what interests them instead of quickly getting dressed as you asked them to. Frustration is often felt when you are trying to clean the house and others who are capable of assisting choose to sit in the middle of a messy room to watch TV or read a book or play with even more toys, adding to what already needs to be picked up.   Frustration is simply not having everything exactly as you would like and wishing but not knowing exactly how to make it different without further frustration or getting involved in a fight. .

Frustration is confusion and discontent.   Anyone of these feelings can and are triggers for anger.

Responsibility and Blame

Responsibility is a trigger feeling for anger. Strong feelings are involved whether we feel responsible or are denying or refusing to take responsibility.

Anger is a defense against feeling our own emotions or taking responsibility for our own decisions, our own results or our own choices. Anger is a tool of blame, a defense mechanism so that we do not have to look at our own selves because to do so would be hard and might hurt. If you can be angry with someone else for upsetting your life, you don't have to admit or take responsibility for the mistake that cost you dearly. As long as you can keep your focus in anger you do not have to feel the loneliness or the depressions or the sorrow you created in your life. As long as you can deal in anger you can fool yourself into believing you still have control over your emotions. You can't work with other people because they represent the result of your choices, so you will be angry with them and fight with them. If the anger is strong enough perhaps they will take the responsibility and you can feel better about yourself.

Taking responsibility for our actions involves feelings that are equally as strong. We have to feel the results either good or bad and make other choices. We may not want to make other choices or have the responsibility for making further choices because we may not feel worthy, smart enough or courageous enough. Facing those feelings brings on other emotions and as they surface anger can sometimes be the way we express our feelings about the pressures of responsibility and accountability.

Sometimes we even take responsibility for something that perhaps we shouldn't have. What seemed like a choice at the time later results in feelings of resentment and disappointment. We find anger growing because the person who should have taken the responsibility left you with the burden to carry or the results that aren't fair for you to receive since you didn't create the circumstances. The disappointment in their not taking the responsibility is disguised as anger at them for not learning the lessons we think they should have. Taking on someone else's responsibility triggers a feeling of guilt for not teaching them properly or not protecting them enough and we mask the feeling behind anger at ourselves. Admitting responsibility for something we had nothing to do with seldom works but it does trigger other emotions.

Identify Your Rewards and Beliefs

Recognize Your Rewards

Once you have identified some of your personal anger triggers you can take some time to look at the rewards you receive for being angry. Honestly think about the rewards you not only give yourself but also others give you. If you are constantly getting angry over and over again, and wish to change your life actions, take a look at what you like about what happens in your life when you choose to be angry.

Does your anger keep you from having to talk or interact with people that do not believe, live or act the same way you do? If you push people away with anger and keep them at a distance you can more easily surround yourself with people who don't question you, offend you or expect you to be any different than you want to be. Surrounding yourself only with those that you can control and manipulate is a reward you give yourself. Choosing to get angry may keep people from expressing their particular observations, opinions or beliefs. Your reward is being able to live in your own little world where you can always be right because there are no other ideas to think about but your own.

Perhaps getting angry is your way of escaping what you think of as unpleasant situations. Choosing to get angry allows you the excuse you need or want to run away from the conversation, situation or incidence. Getting angry with someone for saying something you don't like might make him or her stop the conversation. Your reward is not being asked to listen to something you may not like. Perhaps the anger you have shown on previous occasions gives you an excuse to not talk to someone at all. Your reward is you can hide away from others by saying you can't go somewhere or talk to someone because you "might" get mad. Another reward you give yourself is if you are not present for the conversations or decisions you can play other games you like or which may serve your purposes. One reward game is acting or speaking irresponsibly and expecting others to forgive or forget because you say "I wasn't there, so I didn't know." Another reward game is acting or speaking irresponsibly, expecting others to overlook your actions or accept them, because you can say, "I didn't agree to..." or "I didn't say I would..." or even "It wasn't me that...."

Is the volcanic blowup when you finally yell and scream, rant and rave your reward for all the many times you kept your silence, buried your feelings or chose not to enter into the conflicts? Do you use the unexpected blowup to reward yourself for being the "good" little boy and girl the rest of the time? Do you rationalize that if you don't react to others, don't feel the feelings as they occur, stand back in frustration as others get what they want and you don't or live your life for others instead of yourself that you deserve a big anger blowup once in a while? Who do you choose to reward yourself in front of? Who do you choose to experience your blowup? Is having them see your anger and hurt the higher reward? Is your reward, on a different level, letting them see in one big session just how patient, understanding and loving you have been? Is their sorrow, their hurt or their apology the real reward you are seeking?

What are the rewards of control you give yourself and others because of anger? When you get angry or talk angrily is it because your reward is feeling in control? What is the goal of the anger? Is your reward controlling someone else? Is your reward being the one in control of the situation or event of the moment? Have you ever given, consciously or unconsciously, the reward of control to someone else? Have you ever stomped out of a room in anger and rewarded the other person? Perhaps your goal or reward is getting someone to run after you to express his or her love. How many times have you left the room in anger and then waited a little way off for the other person to come and seek you out to express their sorrow or their love or their obedience? When they come to you is your reward the feeling of power and control?

There are probably as many types of rewards we give ourselves, as there are reasons for choosing anger. Rewards are personal and changing so it is up to you to look for your own rewards. Are your personal rewards worth the prices you pay in time, relationships and feelings of personal worth?

Explore Your Beliefs of Life

Explore your beliefs of life. Ask yourself where you learned them or why you chose them. As a child did you feel you were treated fairly? Based on those experiences what did you choose to believe about life in general? Do you feel that life is fair, that you get the same breaks others do? Do you feel others get more opportunities than you do? Do you believe in the idea of sameness, that everyone should get the same things in the same amounts? Or do you believe in fairness, where people are able to earn more if they work for more? Do you believe you are worthwhile? Do you believe others honor your opinions, your ideas? Do you feel impelled to make believe as you do? Because you believe that you are the only one that is capable of thinking correctly?

What about your beliefs about gender? Do you believe men are better than women, or women are better than men? Do you believe that men and women should be expected to do the same things? Do you believe men and women can do the same types of work or activities? How do you view the stresses and demands of typical male professions versus typically women held jobs? Do you believe a secretary who spends all day thinking about better ways to serve her boss and always being alert to new experiences each day can come home from work just as tired as the man who goes and hammers nails into a wall all day long? Do you believe women were made to serve and honor men or do you believe that a man and wife should work equally together to maintain a comfortable neat home? In your home do you expect someone to clean your clothes, cook your food or do you take turns doing someone else's laundry or making sure that diner is ready when your spouse comes home? How do these beliefs affect the things you and circumstances you choose to get angry about?

What are your beliefs in a God or a Higher Being? Do you feel that life is just a series of fateful events? Do you believe there is a higher being that is omnipotent and eternal? Do you believe your life is already planned out and you are just following a path previously set with no choices in what befalls you Do you believe there is good and evil, light and dark? Do you believe you have obligations to your ancestors to live a certain way, to follow certain traditions and sustain a particular religion or culture? Do you believe in angels and spiritual intervention in your life? Or do you feel like you are all alone in this life to struggle along? Do you believe you must leave others behind in order to get ahead or do you believe you should take others with you as you progress, grow and move from one level of life to another? Do you believe in families or in standing alone? Do you believe in working and pulling together for the betterment of all or do you believe in every man for him? How do these beliefs play into the choices you make to be angry with yourself or others?

What are your beliefs about yourself in comparison to others? Do you find yourself comparing yourself to others and making decisions based on how their perceptions align with your own? One of the most common theories I hear about is the "I'm OK". There are three basic positions that are taken: I'm OK You're Not; I'm Not OK, You're OK; and I'm OK, You're OK. In your relationships with others what do you believe is your position? Is it different with those you love and those you hate? Why? When you choose into anger do any of these beliefs act as a basis or a beginning? How do you feel about being OK or Not OK?

What are your beliefs about anger itself in life? Does it serve a purpose? Who do you allow to be angry in your life? Do you believe it is okay for you to be angry but not for someone else to be? Do you believe anger makes you stronger or weaker? Do you believe

32

people can control their anger? Do you feel anger is an emotion you are entitled to under certain circumstances or in difficult situations? What are your beliefs about how stress affects anger? Do you even believe anger is a problem? Do you believe anger is a challenge you need to overcome? Do you believe you can manager your anger? Do you believe others can manage their anger?

Search your beliefs on life, circumstances, expectations and visions. Ask yourself about your personal beliefs. Explore how these beliefs act as triggers for your anger or feelings you experience with either pleasure or sorrow. These core beliefs you discover will help you to learn more about yourself and the world you create for yourself and others around you.

Experience the Feelings

Whatever the feelings are that trigger your anger, experience the feelings. Don't brush the feelings away as non-existent. Recognize a feeling when it comes. Any feeling can be a trigger, so be aware of your emotions.

The Five Senses

Experience your anger with all of the five senses. Really think about what sensory experiences become parts of your anger. Think about the feelings, smells, tastes, sounds and sights you associate with being angry.

Ask yourself what does it feel like to be angry? How does your body feel? Do your muscles tighten up or do they relax? Do you associate a tight stomach, a headache or a feeling of increased hormones or energy? Do your hands become clenched? How does that feel? What does your skin feel like? Do you feel hot and feverish or do your hands become sweaty even while you feel cold? Are you able to sit still or do you want to stand up to pace or even run away? What does anger feel like? Do you feel the skin of someone else as you hold them, slap them or touch them? Do your hands hurt because your best way to express your anger is to hit something hard?

What sounds come to mind when you think about being angry? Do you hear your own voice? Is it calm or raging? Do you and others speak slowly or talk as fast as possible? Are the voices of those you are angry with sound calm, frightened, timid, controlled or are they also yelling and screaming to be heard or understood? Do you listen to the other voices or are you so focused on making sure you are heard that you don't even hear anyone else but yourself? Do you hear the sounds of children nearby or is there the silence of only two people together? Do you hear other people in the room you are trying to impress with your words? What are the words they are saying to encourage or discourage you from your thoughts or feelings? What are the most common words you hear just before your anger arrives? What are the words you hear that make you choose into anger? What are the words you hear yourself using when you are angry? What words do you hear others using most often when you are angry? What are the words that you want to hear as a result of expressing your anger? Do you hear what you are listening for? What do you hear yourself saying then? Are the sounds you associate with anger the same whenever you are angry or do you associate different sounds with different people in your life? When the anger is over what are the words you hear? What do you hear yourself saying? What do you hear others saying?

Are there smells that you associate with the feeling of anger? Do you smell dinner cooking or the smell of blood? What is the first smell that comes to mind? Do you smell the odors of home or the dirt of the yard? Does it smell like the flowers you wish you had or the ones you got as an apology? Do you smell the cigarette or drugs you had before you got angry or the ones you know you will need after your anger is expressed? Do you associate the smells that come to mind with your bedroom, your kitchen or someone else's home? Do you associate anger with a particular smell, a perfume or spot in your yard? What are the smells you associate with the aftermath of anger? Do you smell food, the freshness of a swimming pool or the scent of flowers? When you get over the anger what are the smells that experience most often? Are the smells pleasant or annoying?

What tastes does thinking about your anger bring to mind? Do you taste the tobacco from a cigarette or a creamy chocolate candy bar? Do you taste a steak, tacos or spaghetti that you associate with eating? Does your mouth feel like it is full of cotton and dry or is it wet with saliva? What tastes did you experience before your anger or what tastes did you miss that helped your anger erupt? When the anger is over what are the taste rewards you seek? Do you taste a cup of coffee, another cigarette, drugs as you get high or the coolness of ice cream melting in your mouth? Do you taste the kiss of forgiveness or the bitterness of regret?

When you think about your anger what images come to mind? What is the first face you see? Who is the face you see most often? What do you see before you, someone who is old, someone younger or someone of authority? Do you see a friend or an enemy? Is there understanding, anger or sorrow in the faces you see before you? What do others look like? What do you look like when you see yourself in a mirror, a window reflection or pictures of yourself you have seen? What are the sights of the room you are in? Are there pictures on the wall or is it a greasy cluttered garage?   Are you in a bar, a home, a car or walking away outside? Do you see your spouse, your mother or your children or your friends nearby? What do they look like?   What are they doing?   Are you apart of it or just an onlooker? What are the colors you most associate with your anger? Is it the color of a shirt you are wearing, the color of the clothes someone else usually wears or the color of a wall in a room you most erupt in?   What are the images that come to mind quickly? Do you see yourself towering over someone or pointing an accusing finger? Do you see someone coming nearer or drawing away from you? What do you see in front of you when you think about your anger? Do you see yourself sitting listening to someone else talk or do you see yourself striking someone?   Do you see the face of defiance before you or one of submission?   When the anger is over and calm is restored do you see the loving face of others as you apologize to them or do they come to you with apology and sorrow in their eyes? What does it look like when you decide to calm back down? Does it look like a park, a secret place in the mountains, a favorite fishing hole or working in a dusty garage working on the repairs you've been putting off? Does it look like a subdued candle lit bathroom or are you now arguing with others? What are you wearing? What are others you see wearing or doing?   Do you see yourself smiling or frowning?

Experience the Feeling Again

Experience the feeling again. Somewhere along your path in life you learned to react with anger. Ask yourself how you learned to feel this way before? Where did you learn it? Who did you learn from? Did you learn that anger was a good way to react as a child or did you learn to use anger to get what you wanted as you grew up? When or where have you used anger before to get what you wanted? Do you still use anger the same way or are your reasons for getting angry different? Where have you felt this feeling before? Think about the first time or even the last time you felt this way? How did it feel as a child when you were angry? Did you experience anger from others in your past? How did you feel when you were exposed to that anger? Experience the times again and feel the hurt, the pain or the relief as the events unfold.   What was going on and why did you choose to be angry? Take time to feel the old pain you had then. What did it feel like? Does your present anger feel the same way? Did you like feeling angry in the past? Do you like feeling angry now? When you felt this way before how did you deal with it? Ask yourself if that decision is still appropriate now? Does your former reaction fit the present circumstance? By recognizing how you chose before you can make a more conscious choice now. Experience the past and the present.   Ask yourself what you learned from your experiences with anger before? Do you want to learn the same lesson, choose the same way or do you want to make a different choice, feel a different way and perhaps get some different results?

Experience Your Beliefs

Experience your attitudes about the way you are feeling. Experience your feelings about your beliefs about anger. Do you believe it is better to be angry than to feel sad, afraid or discouraged? Do you believe that you have the right to be angry about something but someone else does not have the same right? Do you believe that you cannot chose something besides anger while you expect others to do so because they have more experience or because of your relationship? Is it okay for a child to feel anger but not a parent? Do you believe it is okay to express anger through violence or do you believe it must be managed? Do you believe if someone is angry it is okay for them to abuse you and you should take the abuse without regrets or trying to get away? Do you believe it is okay to walk away from someone whose anger is out of control or do you believe it is your duty to stay and listen until they have expressed all of their feelings in whatever way they choose? Do you find you judge yourself harshly or are you okay with experiencing the feelings you have? Where did you create your attitudes and beliefs about feeling a certain way? Is it okay to be sad, to feel hurt or to feel discouraged? These are all real, human feelings. Is it okay to admit to being human or did you somewhere along the line decide or learn these feelings were unacceptable, not be shared or experienced and should be guarded by a show of anger? Did you sometime decide anger was a shield you believed protected you from being vulnerable? Do you believe that your anger protects you from having to listen to what someone else may believe or see? Experience your own beliefs about how to feel and about how you really do feel. Do the two feelings match or are they at odds with one another?

Expressing the Feelings

What stops you from expressing the feeling?

What is it that keeps you from expressing your real feelings? It is often easier to express the feelings of anger than the feelings which are underlying. What are the hurdles you need to jump, the barriers you need to break through, the fears you need to overcome before you can express your feelings openly and honestly, to yourself as well as others? Take some time to ask yourself what the risks are you perceive in expressing your feelings.

Perhaps one of the reasons you do not express your feelings is you are afraid. It is okay to feel afraid. Begin with this feeling, honestly admitting it. Admitting you are afraid and expressing the feeling opens the way for you to find out what you are afraid of, then facing the fear in order to grow or heal. I have many times heard fear defined as "false expectations appearing real." There is another way to define fear that has to do with our feeling. Fear is "feelings of expectation that appear real." Fears are based in experiences and our perceptions of the results we received. They are not always false, because they are often based on a truth. It really did happen once before, we didn't like it and are now afraid of it happening again.

So what are some of the more common fears keeping you and me from expressing our feelings? One of the first is a fear based on trust of others. If you do not trust others fear of their reactions follows naturally. Are you afraid someone will not understand how intense your feelings are and will make light of them? Are you afraid they will not believe you are serious or that you may really feel the way you describe? Are you afraid of someone laughing at you for the way you express a feeling or emotion? Do you ever laugh at or brush off, in the same way, the feelings and expressions of emotion from others? Your fears may be well grounded in the atmosphere of the relationships you have created. Are you willing to risk and create something different by not being afraid?

Are you afraid of looking vulnerable or weak if you express your inner, most tender feelings? Your fears may be well grounded and learned through experience. Others may have laughed at you before, but there are probably just as many times when people may have listened if you allowed them to. If you are afraid of appearing weak or vulnerable, you might have experienced a time when such a feeling had a result you did not like, so you decided to not let that happen again. What are you afraid of if you appear weak? Do you feel you have been taken advantage of when you felt weak? Why is that important to you? What decisions surround your fears of expressing your less than perfect self? What is your personal definition of vulnerable, tender or open? Only you can answer the questions.

Are you afraid of being believed if you express your feelings? What are you afraid will happen if you express a feeling and someone actually believes you? What are the reactionary feelings you are afraid they will have? If you say you are sad are you afraid that they will try to make you happy? Maybe you enjoy being sad. Being sad gives you a reason to stay alone in your home in a world you can keep in control. You don't want anyone to change what you have perfected by introducing something into it, so you avoid the possibility. Are you afraid of telling someone of a feeling because you are afraid they will pity, feel sorry or even try to help you? What would happen if they did? What are you really afraid of? Will their pity or assistance require your thanks or effort on your part? If they offer their help would they expect you to change when you don't want to? Are you afraid of sharing your feelings because if they believe you they might also believe you could desire your life to be different?   Are you afraid of saying you feel like a victim because someone might ask you to make a choice you are not willing to make? Are you afraid that if you are believed and then don't change that those you shared with will then desert you? Has it already happened before?

Perhaps you are among the many who were taught you were supposed to listen but not speak. The old saying of "children are to seen not heard" comes to mind. Did you learn that it was okay for others to feel, talk and communicate openly but it was not a right or privilege you were entitled to?   When you talked about your feelings as a child or an adolescent were you listened to? Did you have friends and parents that cared about what you said or were relationships based in being able to listen to others ideas, feelings and thoughts while keeping silent about your own? Did you learn that the only ideas and feelings that counted were someone else's and yours were not worth listening to? Did you grow up in a home where parents ruled, children listened and feelings didn't matter? Perhaps your own feelings could not be expressed if they conflicted with someone bigger, older or in some authoritative position.

Do you choose to not express your true feelings because you feel they are not of worth? Do you feel your feelings do not count as much as someone else's? Are you one of those people that believe it is more important and more loving to meet the needs and feelings of others than to seek after your own desires by listening to your feelings?   Were you raised with the example that love is always thinking of others before yourself? It may be hard for you to express your feelings because you know they may not match or be the same as someone you love, so you listen to their feelings, try your best to understand and share their feelings instead of expressing or admitting your own. Do you perceive and believe by not expressing your feelings you are showing love and respect?   Many people do. However true love is about honesty, sharing, meeting each other partway and caring about the other person. Love works both ways, if you cannot express your personal feelings are you feeling the love back that you are willing to give away? By keeping your feelings unexpressed are you denying others the opportunity to show you the same kind of love you give them?

Feelings are sensitive and tender, whether they are feelings of joy, sorrow or pain. Sometimes they are buried deep within and kept secure beyond reach. Perhaps you were a child who felt abused, tortured or abandoned. The pain was felt so strongly that you did not want to deal with it and go on, so you put the feelings behind a wall of forgetfulness. You may no longer feel the pain but in order to protect the pain, you made other unconscious choices about trust, love or belief in those around you that affect your life even now. As the walls became thicker and higher, the feelings to be expressed become harder to reach. . If you cannot remember a portion of your childhood, how can you explain why confidence is low or why you feel the need to dull the pressures of daily? Until you are able to break through the walls to the memories protected feelings will not be expressed or wounds healed.

There are also feelings of joy and happiness hidden, even from you, in the same way. Perhaps you once loved, joyfully, full of excitement and hope but put those feelings behind you because of a change in life that seemed traumatic or painful in some way.   The feelings of joy were so precious you did not want to lose them, so you hid them deep behind walls of resentment, mistrust and independence. You may seek to find the missing joy or love through sex, drugs or acting out for attention.   It may take a loving therapist or friend to assist you past blaming others for your unhappiness and expressing the sorrow you felt in choosing to put those precious feelings away.

Learn ways of expressing feelings

Once you have looked at what keeps you from expressing your real feelings, you can take a look at finding ways that work for you of exploring and expressing those feelings safely. Since feelings are so individual and different no one single way of expressing your feelings works. Because there are so many feelings experienced you may find, as I did, you need many different ways of allowing feelings to be expressed. Sometimes it is possible to talk with others whom enjoy your presence. Sometimes you will find you need to sort through the feelings alone before you can adequately share them with others. You may find sometimes just being able to express and recognize the feeling silently to yourself is enough to allow you to move forward, to choose differently or live more peacefully with yourself and those your care about.

Below are just a few ways that have worked for others. Find what works for you. Try several of the ways. Develop your own safe way of expressing the buried feelings. Look beneath the surface of anger, then trust what you find is worth expressing. Surprise yourself with the flow of thoughts you will unleash once you can allow the door of expression to open. .

Make a Note

The safest and most enlightening place to begin is with a blank piece of paper and a pen or pencil. Few people are threatened by or afraid of a single piece of paper. Most people are not intimidated by a single piece of paper. A piece of paper cannot control or manipulate someone in any way. Paper is a safe place to express the feelings you have for it cannot and will not respond with its own opinions or beliefs. Paper silently sits and waits for you to share, receives your thoughts without judgment and doesn't devalue, in any way, your thoughts, words or feelings.

Don't wait until later if you have a feeling pushing to be heard. Any paper will work. What have you got in your purse or wallet right now? Do you have an old receipt you haven't thrown away yet, a note from work you don't need any more or the program from a performance you attended recently. If it has a blank space you are set. What the paper looks like is of little consequence. All you want is a safe blank area to write a single word or a whole page, as time allows.

Allow your thoughts to flow from your heart and mind, through your fingers to the paper. There is only one rule you must follow: Don't censor. Allow your thoughts to simply flow. Whatever comes to your mind express it? If you are angry, then say you are angry. If you are frustrated, then go ahead and write in bold letters, I AM FRUSTRATED. There are no right or wrong ways. Whatever works for you is perfect for you. The important thing is to just do it.

Write a letter

Write a letter about how you feel. The letter can be to yourself or to the person you are angry with. You don't have to mail it or send it. The idea is just to get the feeling out, to express how you feel. In writing a letter you address or focus your thoughts. It is like being able to talk to the person without interruption, misunderstanding or other feelings

Write a letter to yourself. If you could tell yourself anything you wanted to hear, what would it be? Write down how you are feeling, why you are angry. Write down why you think you should or should not be angry or have the feelings you do. Talk about what you would do different if you had the chance to do it your way. Talk about what you would like to hear the people you are involved with. If you are angry with someone, what would you like to hear from him or her instead of what you are hearing? Write a letter addressed to yourself with all the news of everything, good and bad, which is going on in your life. Putting it into words allows you to see it from a distance. Events that seemed overwhelming at the moment appear less monumental when seen as a part of ongoing day-to-day experiences. . Write your letter as a friend to a friend. Be your own best friend by including comments of encouragement and hope. Write the letter as an outside observer. Include a few suggestions and advice that you might give to others experiencing the same feelings or circumstances. . Any way you can think of is right.

Write a letter to the person you are thinking of. Writing a letter is safe because there is no immediate response. Perhaps you are one of those that can write your feelings, beliefs and thoughts easier than you can speak about them. Tell the other person what you feel, what you would like to happen or how you would desire the relationship to be. Get out all the words you are afraid of saying for fear of their reaction or hurting their feelings or making them mad as well. Work through the gamut of your emotions and thoughts.   Tell it like it is. The letter isn't really written for them, it is being written

42

for you as a way of expressing your anger in a safe way without causing more damage to the relationship, without fueling already raging fires. As you write you will find you become clearer on what really are the issues for you. After you have written the original letter you can decide if you want to send any of these thoughts to the other person. Sometimes just taking the time to express the feelings is enough and you decide you don't need to even tell the other person. Other times you may decide to choose parts of your letter to share. You may decide to reword your feelings in order to clarify something you feel is important for them to know. You will know when you finish the first letter what is best for you. Trust your feelings.

Write a letter addressed to you from the other person. What do you think they will say? Give yourself a chance to hear their side or what you belief they would say if they could speak their mind in safety, without fear of retaliation or destroying the relationship. In writing down what you think they are feeling or thinking, you open yourself to understanding and accepting that different people can see things different ways. Allow yourself a few minutes as you write to feel their anger, their feelings. Doing so will help you better understand your feelings, words and actions, do affect others, whether you think so or not. Write every thought you think they have. You could be surprised at what you learn about him or her and about yourself. Don't take this suggestion lightly because it is a powerful tool in understanding both your own anger and the anger of others.

Journal writing

Write in a journal. A journal is a safe place to just let your thoughts roll forth. Like writing a letter, it allows you to go from one thought to another regardless of how much sense it makes. It is a place to just order your thoughts, find out what you want and discover how you really feel. In a journal you don't have to worry about whether anyone else will ever read it. You can express your truest feelings and thoughts because you can be honest with yourself. Open your mind and let the words flow without thought or judgment onto the paper. Don't worry whether it makes sense or follows logic, just keep writing for whatever time you have. The journal doesn't have to be any great book. A spiral notebook works just as well as a bound hardcover book.   A small notebook with only a few lines per page is just as effective as an 8x11" page of notebook paper. It also doesn't matter whether you write every day, once a week or occasionally as the need is there. It is the opportunity to express the feelings that is important. You will find the time to write when it is right for you to do it, so just enjoy the times when they are available. Keep your journals in a safe place. I have gone back many years later and read parts of my journals to find out how I lived through difficult periods of my life. Where did I find the strength, the determination or the desire to move on in a different direction? The words I wrote 10 years ago are as much a help to me today as they were then.

Sharing the feelings

Share the feelings with a friend. If you are dealing with feelings of anger or frustration, then share the feelings with someone you trust. Talk out the feelings with someone you trust to listen with an open mind. Talk to a mirror if the person there is your best friend. Express the feelings, the anger and any ideas for resolution   Sharing with a friend allows you to hear aloud the things that you are feeling. As you speak you hear the tone of voice that goes along with the emotions. Do you sound sad, hurt or frustrated as you speak about your feelings, the situation or the other person? What is the pitch of your voice? Can you calmly talk about your feelings or can you only express them in a voice choked with tears? Do you talk slowly and cautiously, picking your words with care or do your words rush out fast and furiously in a rush? Do you talk with ease or do you mumble every word through clenched teeth trying to control the emotions beneath? Putting your thoughts and feelings into words is half of the solution. Often as you randomly talk about your feelings you will begin to hear yourself verbalizing what it is you would rather be feeling. As you do so, you begin to solve and deal with the feelings on a new level.   If you share with a trusted friend he or she may be able to suggest different ways of thinking about the situation, different approaches to take or share how he or she solved or dealt with similar situations, problems or feelings.

Sometimes it is most beneficial to talk with someone who is not involved in any way. That someone could be a clergy of a nearby church, a therapist at a community center or a counselor at school. These people can listen without emotion. Some of them have skills in assisting you to uncover concealed feelings. A therapist or counselor has knowledge and skills developed to help you break through or drop the walls that protect past feelings and fears so that they can be brought to the light. They may know of skills in coping with the feelings that come rushing through as holes are made in the walls of protection built up throughout the years around pain and injury. Understanding how you were abused as a child enables you to understand why you do not trust people in your present life. A trained professional can assist in helping you learn your anger with your wife and girlfriends is not going to get any better until you can learn to forgive or remember the anger you had with a previous woman over control or issues of love. A professional can help you connect the memories, or the lack of memories, with your actions and feelings of today. A trusted counselor can guide you through steps of overcoming your anger t you have not yet learned. They can assist you in a plan of action, a system of support, all the while giving encouragement and hope.

Communicate a different way

Learn some new ways of communicating in your relationships. Learn a new way of expressing yourself without anger. There are some people who are so used to being angry and expressing themselves in anger it is hard to even conceive of any other way of speaking. Their experiences with love and understanding, calm communication and deep sharing is limited. Even though they do not know how to change, they often yearn for a calmer, more peaceful way of communicating instead of yelling, accusing and fighting. They know they would be happier, but without a basis to start from, they fall back into old familiar or comfortable patterns and habits.

How many times in your life have you heard the old adage, "If you want something different you have to do something different"? How many times have you or I really listened? Truth keeps popping up in life in many old sayings that after being tried and tested are then passed on as meaningful information to come back to over and over again. Today is your chance to take this truth and decide what you will do with it. What can you do differently to manage your anger? How can you communicate in a different way? I have several ideas I can share that have worked for me and for others. Perhaps one of these will assist you in finding something that will make a difference in your life.

Slow down

Slow down in your communications with others. Speak slower. Listen longer. Keep the conversations at a slower pace. Don't rush yourself or the person you are trying to relate with. Allow time for thought before answering. Give silence an opportunity to intrude for brief moments while one or the other of you catch a breath or think about what is being shared. Keep in mind that time is endless so you do not have to say everything you want to or think you need to right now. Another minute, another chance to speak is on its way in just a moment.

Slow down your communications. Learn to let your mind keep pace with your mouth. Sometimes people begin to talk so rapidly their words are coming out faster than their mind can keep up. They often say things they do not mean to. In the midst of anger most people do not think about or even care about what their words will do to themselves, others or the relationship. The person may talk so rapidly the words just spill out without thought, reason or even knowledge. The words come more quickly than the thoughts or decisions about whether this is really what they want to or ought to be saying. The words may be harsh, accusing, painful, hurtful, accusatory or abusive. They find themselves returning later to apologize. They may come back later to say they didn't mean what they said, lying either to themselves or to the other person. They expect the other person to forgive them and to just forget what was said because after all, they were angry and cannot be held responsible. This common belief that anger gives someone the right to hurt, damage and abuse without being held responsible damages the relationship more than even the words alone

Slowing down or even stopping to allow your thoughts to catch up with your mouth allows you to readjust the moment. You may have an outburst of anger and start to yell or raise your voice but slowing down allows you to realize you are out of control and

46

change immediately. You are feeling and expressing anger but slowing your thoughts will allow you to realize it is not that you are angry it is because you are frustrated, scared or whatever the emotion really is underneath. You can quickly stop the anger, admit to the other person you are sorry, explain what you are really feeling and why, closing the door of anger and opening a door to communication and love.

This is one of those things I find I sometimes need to keep working on. After multiple attempts to get a child to do something, I finally raise my voice a tone or two and say something like "I will not say this again. I want you to ...right now." If I slow down I can stop myself in the middle of the moment and stop the change before it goes any further or turns the situation into something worse. I can stop, take a deep breath, seize the thought of what is really going on and instead of yelling explain that I am just frustrated, or I am tired or I really do need them to do whatever it is I asked because of a reason that is important to either me or to them I know about or am concerned about but haven't shared. Maybe I know someone is coming to visit and I want the house clean. A good example is when I come home after a long day at work. I come in and the children are sitting and watching cartoons in the middle of a messed up living room. Their papers from school are all over the floor. There are remnants of after-school snacks on couches and floors and tables. I need to begin preparing dinner so I don't have time to pick up the mess, so I ask the children to pick up while they are watching their show. I ask them 2 or 3 more times through the course of the next hour without any noticeable results. Finally I come into the room, turn off the TV and raise my voice as I tell them if they are not going to clean then they can just take themselves to their rooms for the rest of the night. About this point one of them is starting to cry or looks scared. That is the moment when I have to slow down or stop and let my thoughts catch up with my emotion. It only takes a moment and I can soften my voice, reaching out to hug them instead of yell. Then I can slowly explain I am feeling overwhelmed, or I need the room straightened up before it becomes too messy for anyone to handle alone, or perhaps we only have limited time to clean because there is an activity they forgot they needed to attend that night. Whatever the reason for the outburst, I can request cooperation instead of expecting them to just act because they were told to. I can diffuse the situation quickly by slowing down enough to recognize the underlying thoughts or reasons for the feelings of anger I am experiencing. I can share the feelings instead of the anger

Stop accusing

Stop accusing others. A lot of anger is tied up with accusing others of doing, saying or acting in a way we do not approve of. The angry person often accuses others of faults he sees. An angry person often accuses others of ruining their life or trying to control. He may appear to act as both a judge and jury. Accusing others involves looking for something to be wrong, to be a fault or to be unacceptable. It involves looking for the negative and then making sure that the other person knows or understands how they are lacking or how much they are disliked for whatever particular reason chosen. Being accusatory puts the other person on the defensive and triggers their emotions to come into play. Rather than being accusatory, seek to be complimentary. Instead of looking for the negative character flaws of others, look for the positive character strengths and communicate positive feelings. Instead of accusing someone of controlling your life, thank him or her for his or her concern. Instead of accusing the other person of doing something wrong, challenge them-, encouraging him or her to change a character trait they are working on or would like to change. Instead of accusing the other person of being wrong offer another way of looking at what you think they are wrong about. Instead of telling someone how stupid they are tell them how their actions are perceived by others or by you. Open the space for disagreement without a fight. .

Use "I" messages

In nearly every relationship or parenting class I have ever attended one of the first communication tools suggested is the use of "I" messages. "I" messages are a way of communicating feelings, beliefs or opinions in a way that is less offensive or accusatory towards others. The use of "I messages" takes the focus away from outside and allows you to focus on your own emotions, ideas or feelings. "I" messages are a great tool in opening up your own eyes to what is really happening to you or with you. The basic sentence goes something like this: "When...then I... because..." The trick is to not use the word "you" in what is said. An example of what most people consider an "I" message is: "When you accuse me falsely you make me mad." Start with a simple common phrase of "You make me so mad." Sometimes you be by changing to "When you accuse me wrongly I get so mad." The higher step is to be able to say "When I think I have been accused wrongly I choose to get angry because it hurts if I am not believed".

It is almost impossible to not take some of the responsibility when using "I" messages because somewhere in the statement you have to say how you are affected. Using "I" messages not only changes how the other person sees the situation but also allows you to see the situation in a new light. "I" messages are clarifying statements of feelings or actions. They are explanations not only to you but also to others of what you see, feel, hear or think. Using "I" messages requires you to give up the blame and be responsible for your own thoughts and actions. "I" messages require you to be less judgmental of others and confrontational. Using "I" messages allows one to give up trying to control someone else and allows you to control the person that really matters, you. Conversations become less controlling and more explanatory.

Some teachers have stressed that in using "I" messages you refrain from using the word "you" in the sentence at all because it is then still offensive, accusatory or blaming. I have found that putting down that rule means many people will refuse to or are unable to use "I" messages as a communication tool or in their conversations. What has helped many people is not to avoid using the word "you" but to make sure that you clarify the "you." For instance, instead of saying, "When you lie to me I can't trust you" own the situation by saying "When I think you have lied to me I can't trust you." In the first statement you are still accusing and assuming. In the second sentence you are opening the way for discussion or an answer. When you accuse others outright you often stop the conversation. There is no way for the other person to respond except defensively. Stating your perception allows the other person the opportunity to clarify, to respond or to further explain. It allows feedback. "I" statements are more of a feed back to the other person of what is being perceived rather than a statement of what is real. When two people are involved, nothing is real. Everything that occurs between them is an interaction based upon perceptions, feelings and past experiences. "I" messages clarify the perceptions and different ideas.

Understand first

In his book, <u>7 Habits of Highly Effective People</u>, Stephen R. Covey, PhD., says that the 5th habit we should develop is to seek first to understand, then to be understood. The development of this ability assists immensely in overcoming and managing anger. Seek to understand, then ask to be understood. Seek to understand what the situation is about, how the other person feels and to understand what happened to arrive at where you are. After you have found understanding, then you can be understood. Most people communicate with the intention to be understood, to be heard and listened to. Allowing the other person to be understood first allows them to be able to listen more attentively when you share your thoughts. They feel that if you are already informed then you can better choose their way. The wisdom in listening to understand before you try to be understood, is that you can answer in a more informed, more understanding way. A simple way to explain this idea is to suggest you use your two eyes, your two ears before you use your single mouth. Listen before you speak. Think before you act. Look before you leap. How often have you heard these old clichés? Well, guess what, these old clichés are more than just words, they are truth lasting through years and years of mankind. The sayings are just as true for this generation as they were for all the generations before. Let the other person go first. Look, listen and learn.

Open communication

Communication is a two way street. One-sided conversations are nothing more than speeches, a dramatic presentation of ideas. It is important to use open communication. An open communication invites opportunity or asks for a response. It says that there may be another opinion and you are open to hearing something more, open to discussion. A closed communication is one that gets only one point across and that is the end of conversation. I have said my peace, I have told you what I thought and that is the end. It is how a person shows power or authority but not how someone communicates.

Acknowledge that there may be a different side, a different way of looking at the situation. Whatever it is you think own the thought and allow the other person the right to think about what you have said. Use "I" messages that are open communication and invite a response. Any message with blame or guilt attached never works. There is a big difference between "You stole my children from me because you always want to hurt me," and "I feel like you stole my children from me because I believe you want to hurt me." The second sentence says this is how I feel and allows a possibility the other person may not feel the same way. The real trick is to not respond in anger when the other person gives their opinion or thoughts. Allowing others a different point of view requires the listener to give up judgment and control. That is not always easy for some people. The most important thing to remember is to not close the conversation by saying "You are wrong." As soon as you say those words you have said you do not acknowledge any opinion or vision other than your own.

Keep the lines of communication parallel. Crossed conversations invite dissension. Strive to communicate on the levels of parent-to-parent, child-to-child, adult-to-adult or parent-to-child. I learned this idea of communication while attending a parenting class. There is much more to the idea than I can share here, but the idea that I want to share is that we need to learn to communicate on the levels that are most effective for the communication. In his book, I'm OK, You're OK, Thomas A. Harris, M.D. talks about his concepts and the traits of the Parent, the Adult and the Child. What are common characteristics that you think of with each one of these as they come to mind? On one end is the parent who communicates in should, have to, must, rules, control, and manipulation by guilt or authority. On the other end of the spectrum is the child who communicates from a feeling of being in the center of universe, expectation, excitement, freedom, wants and manipulates through emotion. In the middle is the adult who understands both extremes and has found a balance and harmony and can communicate from that level.   Often in our conversations we choose to step into one of these roles depending on the person we are talking with. Knowing the position of the other person as well as yourself allows you to better choose effective lines of communication.   Being aware of direct and crossed transactions helps in understanding why some conversations work and others do not.

Use Different Words

Communicate in a clearer manner. Find words that are more descriptive of how you are feeling or that better describe the issues at hand. Instead of saying I am angry, say I am frustrated. Instead of saying simply I am angry acknowledge the truth and say I feel resentment, hurt and a feeling of loss. Play a game with yourself and see how many words you can find to describe the real feelings you are having. Stop saying you are angry and start communicating what the true issues are. "I am so angry with you," don't tell me anything except you are not feeling happy with me. However being more open to communication and saying "I feel hurt and betrayed." or "I feel cheated or mistreated," tells me what I may have done I can change or think about.   Tell the other person what it is you are really feeling and you allow them to take responsibility for their own thoughts, actions and results.

Describe the feelings really going on instead of always choosing to simply say "I am angry." Allow the other person to learn and to grow with you. Saying I am angry is like holding onto a secret. If you tell the other person that you are angry, because anger covers so many feelings, they cannot know what they could or might be able to change at another time.   Claiming to be angry is a way of holding onto the hurt, the pain.   If you want the other person to do it differently: next time then you have to let out the secret. You have to tell the other person what can be changed or tell them the results of their actions.   Learn to use other more descriptive ways of communicating what you are feeling.   Instead of just saying I am angry, tell the other person you feel hurt or used.   Instead of saying you are angry say you are feeling rage because of his or her choice of words, action or deed. Take responsibility for letting him or her know that angry for you means you feel backed into a corner, used, abused, forgotten, or mistreated in some way. Instead of saying simply I am

52

an angry with you, take possession of the feeling angry by saying "I don't like when you change your mind at the last minute" or: "I hate it when others change their mind or rethink decisions and then change the plans." Instead of saying "I am angry" say:" I wish I didn't have to" or "I don't like to have to change because of someone else's choices." Communicating the deeper feeling not only allows the other person to better understand, it helps you to see what you may need to work on yourself

Learn the languages of love

Learn to communicate through the languages of love instead of just with your words According to Gary Chapman, author of "the Five Love Languages: How to Express Heartfelt Commitment to Your Mate" every person has a primary language of love, a way they express love and things they see and acknowledge as expressions of love.   Dr. Chapman identifies the five love languages as: Words of Affirmation, Quality Time, Receiving Gifts, Acts of Service and Physical Touch.

Learning to recognize how others show their love will allow you to feel more of the love and support you may have felt you were missing. Family members you may have felt didn't care about you have probably been expressing love in a different language than you were looking for. If they were offering gifts but you were looking for words of encouragement you may not have felt the love expressed. Perhaps some of the frustration that pushes you toward anger is that your love is not being accepted through the language you have been using in the past. . They may be looking for words of affirmation or quality time while you have been expressing love through acts of service (going to work each day whether you want to or not) and gifts (providing for their wants and needs as they are expressed). Anytime people are speaking different languages without understanding what the other person is trying to say frustration and anger are common results.   Learning to speak and respond in the different love languages cannot help but result in better communication of love.

Words of affirmation are spoken love in the form of an unsolicited compliment, a kind word and words of encouragement. Who do you know shares their love for you by giving support and encouraging you to keep trying? Do any of your family members regularly tell you how great you are and what a great job you are doing? How often do you accept, or do you, the compliments as genuine and real? Who is in your life you know responds positively to hearing words of affirmation? How often do you speak in their language?

Quality Time means togetherness and personal connection, not just being physically nearby. It is quality conversation, really listening to one another. Time changes from just time next to each other to quality time when you insert an element of fun together. Do things you each enjoy. Explore new activities together. When someone stops doing something they love in order to spend time with you, even if you are upset, recognize they are trying to speak in this language of love.

Receiving and giving gifts are both a part of this language. The message of love is the gift giver was thinking of you and wanted to let you know. Expense is not the main thing – it's the meaning. A favorite treat picked up on the way home or a card for no reason sends a priceless message. The gift may even be the sharing of talents and interests. You may not like the bugs and spiders your child brings you but the gift of wonder and the sharing of something they find exciting and wonderful is the gift really being given. Patience with a lingering child, forgiveness of wrongs and hurts and the simple words of "I'm sorry," are also gifts of this love language. Take a moment and think of all the gifts you receive and those you give? Who are the people you know who speak this language regularly? Recognize how what you are willing to receive or not receive apply to your choices of how you feel.

Acts of Service are gifts of time and effort. Cooking, washing the car or doing a batch of laundry can be acts of love. Doing something that is helpful to your loved one will be noticed, if it is their language of love. Challenge the stereotypes and be creative. Open your eyes and look for ways to be of service to those you love. Do something for them they would prefer not do but still needs to be completed. What have you seen someone needs done but doesn't have the time to do? Do it for them. Take a look at the acts of service you look for from others. Does what you are looking for and not receiving have any influence on how you choose into or out of anger?

Are you looking for one large act of service and missing the small everyday acts someone is giving? (Are you looking for the clean bedroom you asked for and missing that they swept the porch while they were playing house or pulled the weeds under the trees when they made their clubhouse?)

Physical Touch is a reaching out in love. A hug, a kiss, holding hands, and touch are all ways of communicating love. Physical touch can be a tickle, a pat on the back, a neck rub, a foot message or putting your arm around someone while watching a show. It is the smoothing of a hair, a touch of a hand, kissing a hurt away or putting on a Band-Aid. It might even be a person reaching out to touch your hand or your shoulder in the middle of an argument. They are trying to say even if they disagree they still have love. If you are angry how do you choose to receive the message? Research indicates that positive physical contact is important to emotional health. Some scientists and doctors even say you need at least four hugs a day. What part does physical touch play in your relationships?

It is important we are able to communicate to others through all the languages of love. As we do so, we will find the language the other person responds to the best. Sometimes the favored language may change as life happens along the way or we go through phases together. Right now, one of my main languages I respond to is service. I find myself not needing the physical attention or the words of love as much as I cherish the unasked for assistance or the cooperation of assisting with work without being asked or perhaps a super good job beyond what was asked for. These show me love and mean more to me right now than saying I love you. On the other hand my 5-year-old granddaughter's love languages right now is physical touch and quality time. She expects you to give her everything she wants and is learning to wait for things, learning delayed gratification. But give her a hug and a kiss and she is putty in your hands. She loves hearing you love her, but give her a hug. A tickling session or time sitting with your arm around her while you read a book and she knows you love her as much as you say you do. The best way to let her know I love her is to have her spend time with me or for me to spend time with her. She feels loved when you take the time to play a game or have her help with cooking a meal. I have a granddaughter whose language of love is a word of affirmation.

She doesn't always care about physical attention, but words of praise and encouragement are what she yearns for. She is going through many changes and experiences in her life so knowing she is making the right choices and choosing the best ways of dealing with issues as they arise is important to her. On the other hand, my grandson's present love language is receiving gifts. Nothing influences him better than a reward of some kind, a toy or a gift for good behavior. Not all gifts need to be physical. With him a special privilege or an extra hour of play is as much a gift as a wrapped present. His second language has to do with quality time. He craves attention from others and drives his sisters crazy because he is always trying to do and be wherever they are. Many times his efforts result in losing the time and attention he is seeking because he ends up upsetting them by pushing too hard, being too rough or acting inappropriately to get attention. So he feels loved when I can or will take the time to simply pay attention to him, listen to whatever it is he wants to talk about without any judgments about whether his comments are associated with the present or questions about the past or hopes for the future. Paying attention to what it is he wants to show me at the moment, whether it makes sense or not to me is a way I can speak in his language and build a better relationship.

Forgive and Heal

Find A Way to Forgive

Managing anger requires the gift of forgiveness. Forgiveness is a gift of love, a gift of peace. Forgiveness is a miracle-making tool that will change attitudes, behavior, thoughts and actions. When forgiveness appears faults melt away, anger thaws and healing grows in its light. It is almost impossible to improve a relationship and move forward if you have not forgiven the actions or words of the past. The anger will always get in the way, if not today then perhaps tomorrow. It will stay there waiting to be recognized until you are willing to forgive and choose to feel something different. Move forward in your life by seeking to forgive others.

Forgive others

The first person to forgive is the other person. Forgiveness doesn't begin with the other person asking for it, although sometimes that is what we are looking for. Forgiveness begins with us. Forgiveness begins with recognizing our choice and being willing to make a different choice now.   Forgiveness doesn't even involve the other person. Too often we say we can't forgive someone if they are not there to talk to or because we have broken our ties with them. The offender may no longer even be a part of our lives and yet we still feel the offense and harbor the feelings of anger. Well, guess what, it doesn't matter. Forgiveness isn't even about them; it is about you, the one and only one here.   It is a personal choice that you and only you can make for yourself.   Forgiveness is a choice you must make to let go of the old emotion and choose something different.

Forgiving others doesn't mean forgetting. Sometimes that can be a part of forgiveness. Forgiveness is releasing the hatred, the anger, the blame, finding a peace in your heart towards the other person. Forgiving doesn't mean you forget the lesson. Forgiving means you accept this person aided you in learning a lesson, in learning more about you, aided you in looking at something new, in a new light or growing in a different direction.   Forgiving means releasing the other person to get on with their life without the burden of guilt, pain or always looking over their shoulder waiting for your next move, word or action against them. It is a way of healing yourself.   In forgiving someone you feel may have wronged you or interfered with your plans or beliefs in life you release your own powers to heal your self to feel love, respect, safety or peace. Without forgiveness there is no peace.

I don't kid you. Forgiveness is not always easy. Sometimes it can be but every time it is a step we take alone.   It is easy to change a feeling or to forget a minor offense such as a rude word, a small feeling of neglect or a misperception on the part of another. It is harder sometimes to forgive the deeper hurts that have festered for years such as neglect, abandonment or abuse. These may take a series of minor steps to get through to the final forgiveness.

What is it you perceive this person has done to you?   What damage do you feel they have inflicted? Why do you hold on to the hurt you think they showed? What was their act, action, word or position t you felt offended by? Identify what it is you felt. Did you feel hurt, ashamed, embarrassed, unloved, betrayed, abused, unloved, and powerless, less than, unacknowledged by, left out controlled, manipulated, or just plain offended? What was the feeling you chose to be angry about? Now recognize none of these feelings you just identified belong to the other person. The first step in forgiveness is recognizing the feelings of anger you are experiencing are the ones that you chose and may still be choosing to feel.

Now is an opportunity to make a new choice to feel something different. The trick sometimes is finding or deciding what we want to replace the old feelings with. It make takes a series of choices to ever reach a feeling of love but you can take the first step by choosing an emotion less powerful, less negative than hate or anger. Whether you allow yourself to heal in mini-steps or take a huge leap across a river you thought you couldn't cross is up to you. Just make a choice for something different. Were you offended by something a person said to you in the past? Take the chance to find forgiveness by changing your perception of them offending you to them misreading you. Can you allow the other person to make a mistake? Have you allowed yourself to see them as being someone with a different opinion?

Forget the hurt and accept a lesson. Replace the hurt and anger with a feeling of having learned something about you. If you were offended by someone's comment that they didn't like the way you cooked the meal, instead of being angry about the remark, learn from the experience. You could choose to learn that you can't please everyone every time.

Forgiving the other party with whom you have been angry comes with understanding they may not have done with malice what you perceived. Through your glasses of experience, knowledge, perceptions and beliefs you may have not seen clearly. There may not have been any wrong done and you can easily forgive once you take off the glasses of your perceptions. Did the abuser purposely set out to hurt you or were they fulfilling a need they didn't know how to appropriately act upon? Did the father who raped his little daughter mean to scar her for life or did he want to show his love for

58

her or was it that he could not control his own lusts and desires and needed help he couldn't seek or wasn't willing to look for? Forgiveness means looking beyond our self and allowing possibilities to surface from the bog of yesterday's grief. Replace the perception of hurt with the light of truth and knowledge. Instead of feeling the hurt, forgive and choose into understanding the other person may have been sick, out of control or have simply made a choice that did not work for you or they did not allow you to have a choice in. What about feeling and understanding for the other person? You could feel sorrow for the hurt and pain that caused them to make the choices in their life they have. You could feel an outpouring of love for them as a fellow human being who stumbles through life making mistakes everyday. You might even be able to find joy in simply knowing and allowing the incident to be over, the lesson learned and a chance to begin anew before you.

Sometimes all it takes to find forgiveness is making the decision to allow the action, hurt or offense to be in the past. Remember what happened yesterday may have brought you to where and who you are today, but it is not today. You can't change the past for it is already gone. You can only change what happens from this moment on. Let the past go and move forward to your future.

Acknowledge if you chose to be offended at all you care about the other person's feelings, about how the other person perceives you. Take the feeling and recognize the other person you are angry with is important enough to you to think about on a regular basis. Now ask yourself what you are willing to do to change and get a different result. Forgiveness may take some action on your part. You may have to write a letter. You may have to ask someone else for forgiveness of you in order to heal a relationship. You may get to change something about yourself in order to receive something you desire more.

In forgiving others you may decide you need to meet with the other person and let them know of your forgiveness. Being able to communicate with the person you have been angry with or hurt by and offering your love, forgiveness and acceptance of what happened allows healing in both lives. It offers the other person the opportunity to perhaps ask for your forgiveness or to express their sorrow at the outcome of events. Until you are open to communicating, and remember communication is a two way street, you cannot know what their feelings were or are. It is just as important for them to express their feelings, to recognize their responsibility and feelings about what happened as it is for you. Offering them the opportunity is offering healing for both of you.

Forgive yourself

Forgiving yourself can be even more freeing than forgiving others. Forgiving yourself requires one to admit you are less than perfect. Of course no one likes to admit he or she is less than perfect in every moment yet isn't it exciting to know you are unique and alive. What is the measure of perfection you hold up as who or what you think you must be? At a second glance I bet you would find even what seems perfect on the surface is less than perfect below. Take the example of a diamond that flashes in the sunlight. On the surface it looks perfect, the gem without a flaw. Yet it is the flaw beneath the surface that reflects the light in a unique way and therefore makes it more valuable. So rejoice in accepting your imperfection and forgive yourself.

A huge step in forgiving yourself is being accountable and accepting what you are experiencing is what you have created. It is so much easier for most people to blame others, circumstances or a higher source for where they have ended up, how they are feeling or what they are doing with life. Just like forgiving another person, forgiving you involves a change in choice, a change in perception of the experience and the person involved. It means changing your perception of you in the experience. Are you struggling with feeling you were a victim and cannot forgive yourself for allowing you to be abused whether it was once or time and time again? It is easy to feel that you were the victim of someone else's behavior or choice. It can be terrifying to admit and humbling to say you allowed yourself to be, you even asked for it or accepted the abuse. It is painful enough to feel that someone else has hurt us. It is even a deeper hurt when we know we have hurt ourselves. There is no one else to blame. We struggle to find reasons that may not have ever existed. It may have merely been an experience that we were a part of. Forgive yourself for not taking control when you might have had the chance, for

60

making a choice by not making a choice in the past, for not having control or power over someone else because you were too young to know better or to fight for yourself.

Forgiving you begins with loving yourself for all of your perfections and imperfections. Forgiving yourself involves loving yourself enough to sooth your own hurts, pains and sorrows. Forgiving yourself involves caring about someone valuable it involves caring about you, about what you feel, want, need and deserve.

Forgiving you is love at its deepest form, for it is love of self. Forgiving yourself means loving yourself for all your good and bad, for your strengths and your weaknesses. It is a precious gift to love ourselves for our strengths and the good we bring into our lives. Looking for the good within, the talents and strengths, the good beliefs is an exciting adventure. When you find the good within you forgiveness is like the quake behind a boat, it just follows naturally in the path without thought or effort. When you find the good within, the best parts of yourself you can replace the space where anger has been with joy, belief and hope.

Heal the wounds

Find the beginnings and feel again

Find the beginning of your anger. I talked about finding out what the bottom feelings are. Part of healing is to discover where some of those feelings began and find a way to heal the feelings. You cannot change the past, but sometimes through memories you can revisit the past, re-feel the incidents and find a way to decide to either let the pain go or choose to learn a different lesson. Remember the time when you wanted to be with your friends and you felt rejected. Feel the pain you felt then. It is okay to think about it and heal the pain by feeling what you didn't admit to feeing before. If it helps as you go back go ahead and cry. Cry for the little boy or little girl it happened to. Feel love for yourself and pride in yourself for going through the experiences of the past. Heal the pain by recognizing the strength you had in surviving. Were you abused in some way? As you look back give yourself permission to open the doors and break down a few of the walls you built around the pain. Now go back and love the child that experienced the abuse. What did he or she look like? What was he or she wearing? Look at it as a third person, from a distance until you feel it or see it clearly.   Now put your arms around that child and let them feel safe and loved. Allow the inner child, the lost child of the past, to cry, scream or carry on, to fully express the emotions he felt but couldn't share or wouldn't share with anyone.   Hold that child close and let him or her cry. Give them the opportunity to scream out their hate or frustration. In some instances it helps to provide the inner-child with a means of physically expressing the emotions in a safe manner or in a safe place.   One way is to provide a padded chair that they can hit or a board covered with pillows. Let the child hit and punch out the frustrations. One psychologist I knew kept a child's punching clown in his office as something his patients could safely use to express their emotions physically.

Earlier I talked about using a journal to work through your present anger. Well that same journal can be used to explore the past, to refocus or to express past emotions that are surfacing in the present. Use the journal to explore where these feelings come from, let your mind relax and your hand just write whatever comes to mind. Let the feelings resurface and write them as they come. Let the adult you are now hear the worries and problems of the child in the past. As you write freely, allowing the words to simply flow from your heart and mind to the pages, you will find that you know how to comfort yourself from a new prospective. Years of experience in-between will come to your mind.   You will begin to feel love for the person writing, feeling the pain and the healing blending into new emotions. Continue to write about these new feelings, thoughts and ideas. Believe in the power you have to heal the person that is writing.

Allow the dis-ease to be medicated

Have you ever cut your finger and put a bandage on it to contain the bleeding? Of course you have. We have all learned if we are hurt it is proper and okay to put some medicine on the hurt, bandage it up so it can heal, then go on with life in spite of the injury. We know it might hurt for a little while but if we care for it properly it will heal with time.   As parents we rush to the aid of our children when they are hurt. We wash and soothe the injury, bandage it with care and kiss the hurt away, sending them back out to play and live life again knowing everything will be okay. Do we do the same for ourselves? Why are so many of us afraid to put a bandage on our mental and emotional hurts?

Many of us, if we get a minor cold or the common flu, rush to the store or the doctor to get the newest medications that will relieve the symptoms or medicate the disease. Yet, if we have an emotional dis-ease we savor the pain and discomfort. We allow ourselves to feel the pain much longer than is necessary.

If you are physically ill do you rush to find a doctor that will prescribe an antibiotic or pain reducer, yet refuse to seek for someone who can assist in finding a way to ease the pains that cause you to feel so much anger? If you are not afraid to be seen walking into a doctor's office to get medication to lower your blood pressure, then why might you be afraid to be seen walking out of a bookstore with a prescription on how to deal with the stresses of everyday life? If you are able to stand in a grocery aisle to find just the right over-the-counter medication to relieve the aches and pains of the cold you developed by living your life, then allow yourself to ease the aches and pains of what ails you by looking for a support group, by taking the hand of a friend, by finding a moment of peace to allow healing to begin, to forgive yourself or others for mistakes or impressions. If you are willing to spend money to buy the latest pain reliever for your headaches and body aches, be just as willing to spend a few dollars to go to a class that will enrich your life or even a movie that will make you laugh at life. Next time you buy a box of bandages in case you get a scrape in life remind yourself to be prepared for the scrapes of the soul by having things on hand that you can use to bandage the hurt feelings, the disappointments of life or that feeling of abandonment. Keep a good book handy to read to forget yourself. Keep paper nearby to write a letter to a friend or confidant. Buy a funny movie to watch to change the tears of sorrow into the tears of laughter. Buy yourself your favorite soda and comfort food, along with a box of tissues and keep them for that day when you decide you have earned yourself a good old pity party.

There is no doctor you will find that know you and what you need better than you. Look at the medications that abound on the shelves that surround you. Go ahead and make up your own pharmacy of cures and pain relievers personally designed for you. Be a scientist, always looking for something better, something more soothing and more healing. Trust yourself to find what works for you, then use it often. Medicate yourself and live life with less anger.

Learn the lesson

In a training class I took several years ago, one of the instructors taught a concept that comes to my mind often when I feel like I am in a rut or I seem to be facing the same problems over and over again. The idea he shared is that life is for learning. We each have unique different lessons to learn and life will keep giving us opportunities until we learn the lesson. Some of us learn more quickly than others. Some of us face the problem head on, solve it, learn and go on to the next lesson. Some of us run from the problems as fast as we can, always trying to stay just one step ahead of what even is similar to a challenge. Sometimes the lesson is easy to find, it shimmers right on the surface. Most of the time the lesson is hidden, so most of us get to look for the lessons among the chaos and mess we call problems. If we can look and find the lesson, we can learn. If we learn well enough we don't need to learn the lesson again, but that doesn't mean we don't get opportunities to use the knowledge we learn. If we miss the lesson life will, guaranteed, give us another chance to find it. . Next time the lesson could be harder to uncover. We may get to look deeper or longer. To find the lesson we may need to step back from the issues at hand and take a wider view, a view from outside.

How do we find the lessons? What do they look like? The lessons can be cloaked in all manner of guises. You could learn patience while waiting for a determined three-year-old to dress himself and tie his own shoes even if it takes three times as long as if he just let you do it. You may learn tolerance from a less than perfect six-year-old who insists that his way of making the bed is perfect even if you don't see it as he does. That troublesome boss may be the one you get to work with for no other reason than so you can stretch to your best performances instead of just floating along in your comfort zone. Maybe the reason you get to deal with the car breaking down in the middle of the freeway is so you learn you should have trusted your hunch, your inner knowing, that something

64

would go wrong if you tried to take that trip your best friend asked you not to go on. Perhaps the problem isn't losing your job and being dependent on someone else. Perhaps the lesson is being grateful for the small things you can't lose or learning how to allow people into your life by being a little less independent and accepting gifts of love and service from others whose lesson today could be how to share with others. I have even found occasionally the problem I am facing and solving is there because someone close needs either an example or encouragement in creating a result from his or her own experiences.

Whatever the lesson available or wherever it may be hiding, be open to looking for and finding it. Allow the problems to flow into and through your life encouraging new growth and sprigs of hope, just like a tiny stream flowing through a desert leaves a path of green along its path. .

Silence and Meditation

One of the most important elements of healing is stillness, a time of quiet, of peace, where the frantic movement of elements can slow down, re-gather and work in harmony to heal and mend. Find the silence, the moments in time when you can let healing come. When you envision a hospital, full of recovering patients, do you see the hectic rush of the emergency room, the rushing of doctors up and down the hall, or do you, like most people, think about the solitude and quiet of the rooms? Do you think of the hushed voices, the soft treaded shoes of the staff and restfulness of sleep? In order for the body to heal, we offer it time, quiet, rest and relaxation. We take vacations to escape the hustle and bustle of everyday work life. In order to heal from anger, you need to allow yourself to experience that same quiet.

Experts can tell you all about the many ways to meditate. They can suggest you find a quiet place in your home to be able to sit and think about your spirit or think about a higher intelligence. The yoga master may teach you chants and positions of the body that promote healing and the flow of positive energy. The pastor may suggest finding a place where you can pray in quiet and solitude, even suggesting specific prayers you can repeat. A therapist may assist you in creating an imaginary place of refuge you can visualize with ease, a place representing solitude and joy, where you can escape at will from the outside world. However you decide to "meditate" is a personal decision. Even what you may call meditation and quiet may vary. It is not important how or what you call meditation. What is important is you find something that works for you.

I have heard many people say they don't have time for prayer or meditation. Their days are so busy, filled with stress and activities, they can't set aside a half hour to just sit and think, uninterrupted by children, family, co-workers or demands on their time. I can understand, because I have often felt the same way myself. I can, from experience though, suggest using the few moments we do get in the best ways possible. If you commute to work in a car, you may have the chance to find a minute or two that works. Put on a radio station you enjoy. It doesn't matter whether it is classical, rock, western or the oldies. What matters is for even a few minutes you can allow your mind to float along with the music. Sing along with the tune of just one song. Singing allows you to focus on something or someone outside of yourself. Singing just one song will lighten your mood. Meditation? Others might not call it so, but for many it is as close as they get. If you ride a bus or rail car to work, use those few minutes each day to read a book you enjoy, study a verse of scripture or think about that final kiss from your spouse or children that left you feeling loved. Put a poster on your bathroom wall where you will see it each time you enter. Even a simple little saying, read in the few minutes you allow yourself privacy will allow you to find something different to think about. One man I know taped a card to the underside of his toilet seat. Every time he lifted the seat he smiled as he read "This is your moment of silence. ENJOY." Silly, maybe, but it reminded him to relax and use a moment or two of his life, several times a day to relax and laugh. All of us have at least one minute between the time the alarm goes off and we actually get up and start acting alive. Use that one moment or two a day to just let go of all your thoughts, emotions and feelings. Use that one moment to remind yourself, ": It is a new day." In just those few words you will find the essence of meditation. You will find gratitude, release, quiet, peace, hope and energy.   While taking a shower or bath release any negative energy you are holding onto,

66

letting the water absorb and carry it away. Use these few precious moments to reflect on the positive things you see happening in your life. Use the time it takes to walk from your car to your office to hum a favorite tune, think about the effects of nature around you or reflect on something you would like to accomplish or learn during the day. An old song of the 40s or 50's suggested counting your blessings instead of sheep. It is still good advice today. Before you drop off to sleep, take a few minutes to count anything you think of as a blessing. Allow gratitude to surround you as you drift off into slumber. Don't give up on finding a time of silence or a period of time when you can meditate for a long period of time. Look for, use and enjoy the small moments throughout your day.

Let it Go-

Let it go. Three short little words with the power of greatness. One of the phrases that I often come back to that I learned in an experiential training is to "Let Go and Let God!" I have since read many books that suggest the same thing in different ways. Let go and let the universe proceed is a common suggestion. Let go; let life flow through you and around you, unfettered by feeble attempts to make it look a certain way or end up exactly as you think it should. Let go of the need to be right, to judge or to control. Let go of the emotions that keep you tied up in knots, the feelings of blame, judgment, frustration and revenge. Let go of the pain, the hurt or the memory you experience. Let go of the past, of whatever happened moments ago, yesterday or even years ago.

The idea of letting go is based in a universal law of flow. You can see it in nature. A lake that receives fresh water from streams and rivers remains clear and blue if the water continues to flow downstream leaving again through another river or system of streams or man-made pipes. A lake where the water cannot flow out soon becomes stagnant, green and full of algae. You can see the importance of release when you picture a glass of water. You can fill the glass until it is full, but once full, you cannot add anymore until you have released some of what is already there. In order to receive healing, you need to release or let go of what you are already filled with. .

One way to let go is to give it away to someone else. I agree with many other authors and doctors that there is a humbleness that comes in giving up the emotions and problems to a higher intelligence. It doesn't matter whether you believe that higher power or higher spirit to be a great intelligence, a spiritual being, a resurrected being, a great leader who has previously walked this earth or a God. The principle at the heart is to trust that if you let go, everything will work for a higher good. The principle is to let go, to release the thoughts, emotions and actions being held so arms can be opened wide to receive. You cannot get more until you make room to receive more. You can meditate alone, picturing the higher spirit before you. You might imagine yourself giving him or her your thoughts and emotions as a gift. You can see him or her accepting the thoughts with care, perhaps setting them somewhere safe where they are protected. Some people let go through prayer, either silent in the heart and mind or spoken. They may ask the higher spirit they believe in to take the burdens, the thoughts and the feelings from them. They pray for relief then trust that the feeling of peace will come at the proper time. They let go, let God, and wait.

Another way to let go is to just release your thoughts and emotions to nature and the universe that surrounds us all. Do you believe we are all a part of a continuing circle of life, that nature and we work together? If so you can believe nature is available to us to use, to interact with in a positive way. Just as nature gives gifts of life, it also exists to receive from us. Anytime you want to "Let Go" look around for the natural elements of nature to receive what you are giving away. Here is a simple exercise to try that works nearly every time. Take a deep breath of fresh air. Now imagine the air inside is attracting all the negative elements residing in your body. Hold your breath for a minute or so then slowly breath out, letting all the negative emotions and perceptions escape with the breath. Feel the air leaving you, making room for more. Now once again take a deep breath and feel new energy entering and refreshing your whole body. Water is an excellent conduit of energy. Let go by allowing some of your energy to be released into the water while taking a bath, doing the dishes, playing in a puddle of water with your child, or putting your hands in the spray as you water your flower garden. Just allow it to flow from your fingertips from wherever it comes

68

from in your body. Another exercise I have found helpful is to stand still, feet placed firmly on the ground. Release any negative feelings or thoughts you want to let go of. Now let the law of gravity work. Feel the released elements of life fall to the ground where they become part of the ground you are standing upon. Then walk away, leaving what was released, let go of, behind you.

One other way of letting go is to declare it. Repeat aloud whatever you want to let go of. It might sound something like this: "I willing release my desire to control," or "I willingly let go of feeling the hurt of loss."   Say it aloud, listening and believing. You might want to repeat it several times until you know it is true.   If you feel silly, speaking aloud, then use the power of words by writing down your declaration, reading it silently until you feel what you wrote is real.

However you decide to let go, practice the principle of release often. Let go of what you are now filled with so you can create the space for healing thoughts to reside.

In Conclusion

Continue to Learn

Continue to learn. Learn something new. Relearn something old. If something you have learned doesn't work well for you after giving it an honest try, then look for something else to learn.   There are opportunities for learning new skills and ways and communication tools in libraries, support groups, books, and tapes or at your local schools. Find something you enjoy learning. Learn something you wanted to learn as a child and haven't done yet. Sit with an older friend or relative and allow them to teach you a new skill such as embroidery, knitting or perhaps carving or drawing.

Learn the skills of how to heal the past and the beginnings of your trigger feelings by learning from others.   Join a support group and support each other as you look at old pains together. Find a friend whom you can share it all with. The healing comes in facing the feeling not in hiding it. Just talking about the beginnings will cause healing to take place.   Some people feel they need the assistance of a guide, someone such as a trained professional who can ask the questions that will start to break through the walls. Particularly if someone is afraid of their reactions, they may feel they can be more in control with a trained professional than if they try to heal themselves alone.   Some people may be afraid of the reaction they fear they may have and want the safety of a control nearby, someone who can pull them back if they need it, someone who can lock the door so they can't run away from the problem or the feelings again as they have so many other times. Perhaps what is needed is someone to tell the person seeking healing they are not reaching far enough, someone who can from a distance guide them through the process step by step.

Some people are strong enough to learn from books how to heal themselves. There are excellent books out to guide one through all the steps of healing the dis-eases of the mind and body. Some of these books offer the same advice and steps used by professionals. There are all kinds of books written by professionals on how to meditate in order to find peace, or how to create a sanctuary within your mind where you can go and feel safe in expressing desire and inner wants.   There are books on how to find and love the inner-child; to nourish him or her with the love he or she is craving from you.   There are books designed to help identify the bricks of the walls before you that keep out others. These books can help break down the barriers you may hide behind one brick at a time. Whatever you are feeling, be assured, someone else has already been there before you to prepare a stepping stone for you to walk on.

Take One Day at a Time

Take one day at a time. Life will bring you another day tomorrow, so if you don't find perfection in yourself or someone else today, look again tomorrow. If you slip and fall today, get up and try again today and tomorrow.   If you allow yourself to choose into unwanted anger today, forgive yourself and allow tomorrow to come. Just because you chose to be angry today doesn't mean you will tomorrow or that you will even have the opportunity tomorrow. Keep in mind whatever happened is just a moment in time. A

70

moment that is gone, one you can learn from and move forward from. Each moment, whether one of joy or one of anger, is a new moment. Every moment whether filled with joy or with sorrow is the first moment in a new future. It is the beginning of what is to happen next.

Managing your anger is a day-by-day opportunity or challenge depending on your point of view. I have a grandson that right now is working on controlling his reactions. He makes a lot of choices he already knows the consequences of but he gets mad at himself and others when those consequences occur. He may control his anger appropriately the first two times he is sent to his room or asked to do something someone has told him is unfair but the third or fourth time it happens he chooses to not use his judgment and chooses instead to react violently and with anger. He wants someone, sometimes himself alone, to know he is not happy and doesn't like the results created for him to experience. He tries to change reality by throwing a tantrum, expressing his anger in unacceptable ways and ends up choosing something he dislikes even worse or having his time of denied privileges or alone time extended even further. His only hope at this point is he knows tomorrow will come again and he might choose differently tomorrow.

Don't give up on yourself. You are not a finished product; you are a work in progress. Remember the old cliché, "Rome wasn't built in a day." Give yourself time to change, to grow, to learn and to choose again. You are your own best cheerleader. Cheer yourself on as you head forward. Get excited about possibly making that touchdown. Hear your own voice screaming with excitement as you cross one more finish line.

Find a way to remind yourself to make one improvement or change each day or to work on one particular personal trait each day. Make a card you keep in the car that says, "Smile" and then every time you see that card follow the directions, let a great smile show. Tape a reminder to your front door to breathe as you go outside. Take a deep breath of fresh air and let the stresses, frustration and tension go as you breath it back out. Tape a little cartoon to the bathroom mirror to remind yourself to laugh at least once a day. Laughter breaks up the anger. It gives you a moment of feeling beyond the hurt. Laughter is one of the best healing tools there is.

Medical science has done many studies on the effects of laughter. Medical science has proven that patients who laugh heal twice to three times faster than those who don't. .

Try and then try again. Remember there is no such thing as failure. Failure is only your perception of how you think things should be. If an idea does not work today, try something else tomorrow. If you did not do as well as you wanted to or thought you could, try again. If you did well this time, try again. Do what works to make you feel good, and then do it again. If you think of something new to try test it out today, tomorrow and the day after until it works exactly right for you.

Contact:
Linda Chatelain
Linda@write4now.com

Other similar books by Linda include:

Bridge of Skills

Loving Parenting

www.ingramcontent.com/pod-product-compliance
Lightning Source LLC
Chambersburg PA
CBHW060655030426
42337CB00017B/2626